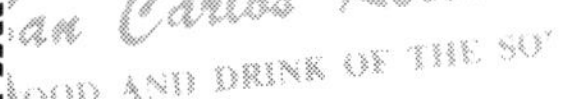

BiTE of SEATTLE COOKBOOK

volume VIII

Printed in the United States of America
Published by I.P.I. Publishing
10245 Main Street, Suite 8-3
Bellevue, Washington 98004
(206) 454-8473

ISBN 0-939449-08-0

For additional copies write to
I.P.I. Publishing
or use order forms provided
at the back of this book.

Judith Deak
Gretchen Flickinger
Publishers

Gretchen Flickinger
Cover Design, Production

Abraxas Typesetting
Typesetting

Overlake Press
Printing

Dee Cundy
Inspiration

table of contents

Dedicated To
Rose Deak and Connie Flickinger
Two Fine Cooks

ALI BABA

707 E Pine
Seattle, Washington 98122

The Ali Baba Restaurant owned by Anwar Aboul Hoss is the first Mediterranean restaurant started in Seattle. The Ali Baba is open every day from 11:00 A.M. to 10:00 P.M.

The Ali Baba is a family restaurant. Impressive, delightful Lebanese specialties, excellent fresh food in an atmosphere of animated hospitality. Try the shish kabob with the special famous lentil soup, shish tawook, and more. Try it, you'll like it! Welcome to Ali Baba.

shish tawook

Serves 4

1 whole chicken, cut into small pieces
1 head garlic
½ Tbsp salt
1 cup lemon juice

Cut the chicken into small pieces. Peel garlic cloves and mash with salt; add lemon juice. Combine garlic mixture and chicken in shallow container and marinate for at least 2 hours. Remove chicken from marinade and wipe dry. Charbroil chicken until well browned and cooked through. Serve hot.

vegetarian stuffed grape leaves

Serves 4 to 6

1 cup uncooked rice, washed
1 bunch parsley, minced
1 onion, sm dice
2 tomatoes, sm dice
½ Tbsp mint, minced
1 tsp salt
½ tsp pepper
1 jar grape leaves

Combine rice, vegetables, and spices in mixing bowl.

Pat dry and spread flat the grape leaves.

Place 1 - 2 Tbsp filling on near edge of leaf. Fold sides toward center. Roll from rear edge to opposite side, enclosing filling. Repeat until all filling is used.

Place in steamer, cover and cook 30 - 40 minutes. Serve hot with lemon wedges.

Edmonds Marina
456 Admiral Way
Edmonds, Washington 98020
(206) 771-4400

Anthony's Beach Cafe is the newest waterfront restaurant of Anthony's Restaurants. Opened in 1992, this casual neighborhood restaurant is located in the Edmonds Marina. The fun, beach-themed atmosphere encourages families and frequent diners to "come as you are." Views of the Olympic Mountains. marina boat traffic and the Kingston ferry all add to the activity of the restaurant.

Fresh Northwest seafood is the specialty of Anthony's Beach Cafe. Anthony's has built its reputation upon offering only the finest, fresh Northwest seafood available. They own and operate their own seafood company for the sole purpose of supplying their restaurants with the freshest premium fish and shellfish. At Anthony's Beach Cafe, you will find this wonderful Northwest seafood prepared in exciting and fun dishes as Fish Tacos, Seafood Chili and Ling Cod Stew. Traditional recipes are given a new twist in the Oyster Caesar Salad or Island Fish Burger. Fresh fish selections in season include Wild Chinook Salmon, Alaskan Halibut, Ling Cod, Northwest oysters, clams and mussels.

Anthony's Beach Cafe serves lunch and dinner seven days a week.

manila clam stew

Makes 2 lg or 4 sm servings

1 pint cream
¾ c clam juice
½ lb red potatoes, steamed and cut into 1" pcs
2 tsp finely diced cooked bacon
2 Tbsp finely chopped leeks
¾ tsp minced fresh garlic
1 lb fresh Manila clams, scrubbed clean
24 ea Pepperidge Farm goldfish crackers (cheese flavor)
2 dashes tabasco
2 tsp finely chopped parsley

Place clams, clam juice, garlic and cream in large skillet or pot. Cover and steam just until clams are open. Remove lid. Add potatoes, leeks, and tabasco and reduce for a few minutes. Pour into warm soup bowls and top with bacon, parsley and goldfish.

This delicious dish is warming; not too heavy. The addition of the goldfish crackers makes a whimsically unique presentation.

peanut butter pie

Serves 8

1 ½ c whipping cream
¾ c sugar
1 Tbsp vanilla extract
6 oz warm chocolate sauce (your favorite recipe or brand)
8 oz cream cheese (room temperature)
1 c creamy peanut butter
Crust:
2 c Oreo Cookie crumbs
4 Tbsp melted butter or margarine

Process cookies in food processor until they are crumbs. Add butter and process until well mixed. Evenly distribute and pack crumbs in a nonstick pie pan and bake at 350 degrees for two minutes to set crust. Place in freezer to cool completely. Meanwhile, whip cream to soft peaks. Set aside. In mixer, beat cream cheese until smooth. Add sugar and mix well. Add peanut butter and sugar and mix until fluffy. Fold in whipped cream.

Pour into pie shell, mounding in the center and smoothing surface. Freeze for one hour. Pour slightly warmed chocolate sauce over pie. Store in refrigerator.

Edelweiss Chalet
225 NE Gilman Blvd
Issaquah, Washington 98027
(206) 392-6652

Here at the Edelweiss Chalet, we pride ourselves on using the finest ingredients available to create many tempting varieties of confections. Next to American favorites, you will find traditional European candies hand dipped exclusively in rich Swiss chocolate.

Boehm's chocolates may be ordered and sent anywhere nationwide from our mail order list.

Visit our factorty. Just minutes from Seattle and Bellevue. Take exit 17 off I-90.

chocolate chip cookies

2 ¼ c flour
1 tsp baking soda
½ tsp salt
1 c butter
¾ c sugar
¾ c brown sugar
1 tsp vanilla
2 eggs
12 oz Boehm's chocolate chips

Pre-heat oven to 375°. In a medium bowl, stir together flour, salt and baking soda. In a large bowl, beat butter for 1 - 2 minutes. Gradually add sugars until well blended. Beat in eggs, water and vanilla.

Mix in the flour combination. Add chocolate chips (plus chopped nuts if you like).

Drop rounded teaspoonfuls on cookie sheets and bake for 8 - 10 minutes.

Cafe Kim

-¦- Vietnamese Food -¦-

458 Hardy Avenue SW
Renton, Washington 98055
(206) 271-7390

singapore noodle

Serves 2

4 oz bean sprouts
2 oz green onion (cut into 2" pcs)
½ tsp salt
½ tsp sugar
1 tsp curry powder
1 Tbsp salad oil
3 oz BBQ pork
½ lb rice vermicelli

Soak rice vermicelli in hot water about 15 minutes until it becomes soft, then drain.

Cut BBQ pork into thin strips.

Heat oil in the wok. Add green onion and BBQ pork, then stir fry until heated through. Add rice vermicelli and bean sprouts. Stir-fry 2 - 3 minutes. Add sugar, salt and curry powder. Mix well.

beef with oyster sauce

Serves 2

1 green pepper, sliced
¼ yellow onion, sliced
½ lb sliced beef
1 Tbsp oil
1 Tbsp oyster sauce
1 Tbsp cornstarch mixed with a little water
¼ c of water
(you can add a little mushroom, water chestnut, baby corn, etc...)

Heat oil in the wok until hot. Add beef and stir-fry until almost well done.

Add onion and green pepper one at a time, frying each 2 - 3 minutes.

Add water and oyster sauce. When mixture comes to a boil add cornstarch and mix well, cooking until sauce is slightly thickened.

Serve with steamed rice.

CAFELOC

407 Broad Street
Seattle, Washington 98122
(206) 441-6883

Seattle Center Food Circus
305 Harrison Street
Seattle, Washington 98109
(206) 728-9292

Cafe Loc is a family operation which was started in 1978 at the 407 Broad Street location. In two years this location had to be tripled in seating capacity in order to accommodate customers during both lunch and dinner hours.

In 1981, a fast food operation featuring the most popular Cafe Loc dishes was established in the newly remodeled Center House at Seattle Center. Both locations continue to enjoy an increasing customer base, and Cafe Loc has consistently received excellent reviews from critics throughout the Puget Sound area.

A veteran food vendor at numerous street fairs since 1978, Cafe Loc is a familiar sight at the annual gatherings of University District Fair, Folk Life Festival, Fremont Fair, Heritage Festival, Bite of Seattle, Taste of Edmonds, and Bumbershoot.

We provide interesting ethnic food and quality at reasonable prices and always with the service style of experienced professionals.

ginger shrimp

Serves 2

½ med onion, thinly sliced
1 clove garlic, minced
2 slices ginger root, cut in thin strips
10 fresh med shrimp, shelled & deveined
5 straw mushrooms, halved
1 c bok choy, sliced, or vegetable of your choice
½ c chicken broth
1 pinch hot chili powder (optional)
½ tsp fish sauce
1 tsp soy sauce
sesame oil
2 tsp oil
1 tsp cornstarch
1 tsp water

Stir fry onion, garlic and ginger root in oil until fragrant. Add shrimp and fry until lightly cooked. Add mushrooms and vegetables, cook until tender-crisp.

Season with fish sauce and soy sauce. Add chicken broth and a few drops of sesame oil.

Dissolve cornstarch in water and add to shrimp mixture; cook until sauce thickens slightly.

Serve hot with rice.

garlic chicken

Serves 2

5 lg cloves garlic, minced
¼ med onion, sliced
1 c chicken meat, cut into strips
½ c straw mushrooms
1 c napa cabbage, cut in bite size pcs
1 Tbsp soy sauce
½ tsp fish sauce
½ c chicken broth
1 Tbsp oil
green onion, cut into 2" long pcs
sesame oil
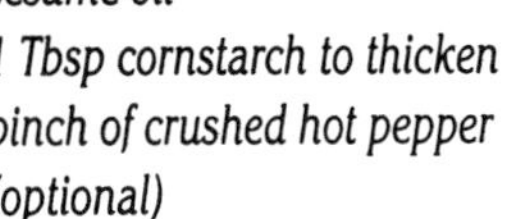
1 Tbsp cornstarch to thicken
pinch of crushed hot pepper (optional)

Fry garlic and onion in 1 Tbsp oil until fragrant. Add chicken and fry until almost done. Add mushrooms and napa cabbage, and stir fry with chicken.

Season with soy sauce, fish sauce and hot pepper. Add chicken broth and mix well. Then add a few drops of sesame oil.

Mix 1 Tbsp of cornstarch with 1 Tbsp water. Wait until the chicken-vegetable mixture is boiling, then pour cornstarch liquid in to thicken the sauce.

Add green onion. Serve hot with steamed rice.

2726 East Cherry Street
(Corner of ML King Jr Way & E Cherry Street)
Seattle, Washington 98122
(206) 323-4330

Since 1985, a warm, friendly Southern hospitality is the atmosphere that greets you at this fast food restaurant where catfish which is "farm-raised" in large freshwater ponds is the specialty.

The catfish can be purchased whole, fillet, fillet bits or cajun style.

Other entrees include red snapper, buffalo fish and seafood gumbo. Dinners include an array of soul foods such as mustard greens, beans and rice, potato salad and a great coleslaw.

Catfish Corner's hamburgers, hot wings, prawns, melt-in-your-mouth hushpuppies and "Rosie's" homemade tartar sauce are huge successes.

"Auntie's" Famous Peach Cobbler is a must, and is a great late night snack.

Catfish Corner is open seven days a week. Food can be purchased to go or eaten in the homey, come-as-you-are restaurant. All of us at Catfish Corner are dedicated to making your visit memorable.

Try our catfish and if you like it, tell a friend, and if not, tell us! Our hours are: Monday to Friday 11:00 AM till 10:00 PM; Saturday 12:00 noon till 10:00 PM; Sunday 12:00 noon till 7:00 PM.

low-cal creamy potato salad

Serves 6

2 lbs new potatoes or small red-skinned potatoes
water
1 tsp salt (optional)
2 hard-cooked eggs, chopped
2 scallions, sliced or chopped
2 stalks celery, chopped
¼ c chopped pickle or relish
½ c low-fat mayonnaise
½ c non-fat plain yogurt
1 Tbsp prepared mustard
1 Tbsp chopped fresh dill
¼ tsp ground white, black or cayenne pepper
several lettuce leaves
optional garnish: fresh dill sprigs

Scrub potatoes thoroughly; cut away deep eyes. If desired, peel potatoes.

In large pot, combine potatoes, enough water to cover, and salt (if desired); bring to boil. Cook on high heat until tender, about 20 to 30 minutes (do not overcook); drain.

When cool enough to handle, quarter potatoes.

In a large bowl, combine potatoes while still warm with eggs (if desired), scallions, celery and pickle to allow flavors to blend.

In small bowl, blend mayonnaise, yogurt, mustard, dill and pepper. Stir dressing into potato mixture; toss gently to coat.

Line salad bowl with lettuce leaves or arrange leaves on plates and top with potato salad; garnish with dill.

Serve chilled or at room temperature.

This weight-conscious version of the ever-popular salad goes well with grilled poultry and fish!

blackened red snapper

Rinse fillets with cold water. In blender container or bowl of food processor, combine bread crumbs and seasonings; process a few seconds to blend.

Empty into shallow dish or onto waxed paper.

Brush both sides of fillets with oil. Dredge fish in seasoning mixture until evenly coated.

Heat large skillet until a drop of water sizzles in it. Arrange fillets in single layer; cook, turning once, until crisp and blackened, about 3 to 4 minutes on each side.

Fish is ready when it flakes when tested with tip of knife.

Serve with lemon or lime wedges.

Serves 4

4 fresh or thawed red snapper fillets (about 4 oz ea)
2 Tbsp bread crumbs
1 tsp garlic powder
1 tsp ground black pepper
1 tsp red pepper flakes
1 tsp dried basil
1 tsp dried thyme
½ tsp cayenne pepper
½ tsp ground sage
½ tsp paprika
½ tsp salt (optional)
1 Tbsp corn or vegetable oil
optional garnish: lemon or lime wedges

Catfish or pompano are tasty alternatives to the snapper in this Louisiana original. Be sure the kitchen is well ventilated when cooking blackened dishes. This recipe can easily be prepared outdoors in a cast-iron skillet placed on or over hot coals of a grill.

zucchini and corn medley

Serves 6

2 Tbsp vegetable oil
2 med zucchini
1 sm red bell pepper, seeded, cut into strips
1 sm yellow onion, chopped
2 c sweet corn kernels, freshly cut from cob (about 4 ears), or canned or frozen
1 Tbsp chopped fresh basil
1 tsp chopped fresh thyme
1 tsp chopped fresh oregano

In large skillet heat oil; saute zucchini, bell pepper and onion until crisp-tender, about 5 minutes.

Stir in corn and seasonings; cook 2 to 3 additional minutes.

15600 NE 8th
Crossroads Mall
Bellevue, WA 98008
(206) 641-0500

Located in the heart of Bellevue, Chili's Grill and Bar is a front runner in casual dining. Chili's offers a variety of Southwestern cuisine such as fajitas, barbecue ribs, quesadillas, Monterey chicken, and super nachos. We also offer an assortment of salads and burgers as well as a children's menu. At Chili's we are dedicated to offering a high quality product at a good value. Join us in the dining room or in our full service lounge for fast and friendly service.

monterey chicken

Serves 1

1 8-oz boneless chicken breast
3 Tbsp BBQ sauce
2 slices of crisp bacon
¼ c shredded jack cheese
¼ c shredded cheddar cheese
¼ c diced tomatoes
1 Tbsp diced green onions

Preheat oven to broil.

Place the chicken breast on the barbecue. Cook approximately 3½ minutes on each side. Chicken should be juicy, but show no signs of pink color.

During the last minutes of cooking on the second side, spread barbecue sauce over top of breast.

Remove fully cooked breast and place on a cookie sheet or metal pan. Place bacon across the chicken in an "X" pattern. Evenly distribute shredded jack and cheddar cheese over the bacon on the chicken breast.

Place chicken under the broiler in your oven until cheese is melted (approximately 1 minute).

Remove the chicken from the oven and place on plate. Sprinkle diced tomatoes and diced green onions over the melted cheese and serve.

Suggested side dishes: corn on the cob, mashed potatoes, barbecue beans or a fresh garden salad.

chicken frisco salad

Serves 1

1 c cubed boneless chicken
⅛ c diced celery
¼ c mayonnaise
1 Tbsp dijon mustard
4 Tbsp honey mustard dressing
⅓ c diced tomatoes
½ c alfalfa sprouts
¼ c diced hard boiled egg
1 Tbsp sliced green onion
1 Tbsp sliced almonds
mixed salad greens

Pour the honey mustard dressing over the top of a desired amount of mixed greens. Toss and place on serving plate. Distribute the alfalfa sprouts over the lettuce.

Combine celery, mayonnaise and mustard in small bowl. Mix well. Add the cubed chicken to the mustard-mayonnaise mixture. Place on top of the sprouts. Sprinkle salad with diced eggs, tomatoes and almonds.

Redmond, Bellevue, Lake Forest Park,
Lynnwood, Edmonds, Federal Way and Olympia

Coco's Bakery Restaurant offers a variety of breakfasts, lunches and dinners. Renowned for our hearty homestyle cooking, as well as our fresh, light fare, Coco's is the perfect place for a fun family gathering or business meeting, as banquet facilities are available. Our pies are fresh baked daily and available for dine-in or carry out. Don't forget us when planning your holiday parties!

strawberry cream cheese pie

Makes 2 pies

2 lbs Philadelphia cream cheese
4 eggs
1 lb sugar
4 oz sour cream
2/3 tsp pure vanilla
2 tsp lemon puree
2 9" graham cracker pie shells
1 lb fresh strawberries in glaze
whipped cream
2 graham cracker pie shells

Mix sugar and cream cheese until smooth. Add sour cream. Slowly add eggs. Keep your bowl well scraped. Mix well.

Combine lemon and vanilla and add to the above. Fill graham cracker pie shells and cook for 45 minutes at 300° F.

Allow pies to completely cool before topping. Place 8 oz of fruit in the center and top with whipped cream.

4549 University Way N.E.
Seattle, Washington 98105
(206) 632-4700

The Continental Greek Restaurant, one of Seattle's oldest continuing Greek eateries since 1967, specializes in traditional Aegean cuisine, but with Greek Isle and health-food influences.

Owner and chef George Lagos prepares well-known Greek dishes such as Spanakopita, Souvlaki and Horiatiki Salata, as well as his own creations, such as Marinated Chicken and Oregano with Pasta and Sauteed Lamb with Herbs and Spices.

The Continental also believes in the superiority of healthy, nutritional foods, free of chemicals and preservatives.

horiatiki (village) salad

In large bowl, combine tomatoes, cucumber and onion. Gently toss with olive oil.

Divide salad among serving plates. Garnish each plate with sliced eggs, feta cheese and olives. Sprinkle each serving with oregano.

Serves 4

2 fresh tomatoes, cut into 8 wedges ea
1 sm cucumber, peeled & sliced
1 sm onion, halved and thinly sliced
Greek-style olives
½ lb feta cheese, cubed
2 hard-boiled eggs, sliced
3 Tbsp olive oil
oregano
salt
pepper

Note: additional olive oil can be added to taste

taso's greek rice salad

Serves 2 - 4

1 head romaine lettuce
1 tomato, sliced
2 c cooked rice
½ c crumbled feta cheese
handful raisins
3 Tbsp olive oil
oregano

Wash and chop lettuce. Put into large salad bowl. Add tomatoes to bowl. Pour in olive oil and gently toss. Add cooked rice, feta cheese and raisins; toss gently. Sprinkle a little more olive oil over salad. Sprinkle with oregano.

635 Elliott Avenue West
Seattle, Washington 98119
(206) 284-7220

Since 1918, your local Darigold Dairies have been making a wide variety of delicious dairy and ice cream products for the Northwest. Now we'd like to share with you two recipes from our very special collection of Darigold recipes, published in our 75th Anniversary Cookbook. Our Anniversary Cookbook includes past classics and present day favorites, from yummy desserts to lowfat appetizers and everything else in between. Thank you for a great 75 years.

beefsteak tomato & monterey jack salad

In a 9" glass pie plate arrange nuts evenly. Microwave on high 1 to 2 minutes or toast in a 350° F. oven 5 minutes. Set aside.

In a medium bowl stir together oil, vinegar and pesto powder. Lightly mix in tomato, garlic and cheese. Season with salt if desired. Cover and refrigerate 1 to 2 hours.

Just before serving time bring to room temperature. Arrange lettuce on 6 individual plates or in a salad bowl. Spoon equal amounts of salad onto lettuce. Garnish with nuts.

Serves X

2 Tbsp pine nuts or slivered almonds
2 Tbsp olive oil
3 Tbsp red wine vinegar
2 Tbsp dry packaged pesto sauce mix
2 lg, firm-ripe beefsteak tomatoes (about 12 oz ea), seeded and chopped
2 cloves garlic, minced or pressed
4 oz Darigold Lowfat Monterey Jack Cheese, cut into ½" cubes
salt (optional)
butter lettuce leaves, rinsed and chopped
freshly ground black pepper

This recipe is excerpted from the Darigold 75th Anniversary Recipe Collection. If you would like to order a copy for yourself or as a gift, send $6.95 (checks only please) to:

Darigold 75th Anniversary Cookbook
P.O. 79007
Seattle, WA 98119

darigold 75th anniversary cake

Makes 10 servings

1 pkg white cake mix
4 c Darigold After Dinner Mint ice cream, softened
2 c Darigold Peppermint Candy ice cream, softened

Whipped cream frosting:
3 c Darigold Whipping Cream
3 Tbsp powdered sugar
2 Tbsp vanilla extract

Bake cake according to package directions for two 9" layers. Split each layer in half. Place bottom cake layer on a serving plate; spread top of layer with 2 cups of After Dinner Mint ice cream to within ½" from edge. Top with second layer of cake. Spread second cake layer with 2 cups of Peppermint Candy ice cream. Add third cake layer; spread with remaining After Dinner Mint ice cream, and top with remaining cake layer. Freeze until firm.

Whipped cream frosting: beat whipping cream at low speed with an electric mixer until thickened; add sugar and vanilla, beating until firm peaks form.

Spread whipped cream frosting on top and sides of cake. Cover and freeze up to 12 hours, if desired; let stand at room temperature 15 to 20 minutes before serving.

15600 NE 8th Street
Bellevue, Washington 98008
(206) 641-4352

About our name: EBRU is a traditional Turkish art. Little is known about the origins of the art of EBRU or marbling. The oldest known example of EBRU, whose practitioners today are precious and few, dates back to 1554.

The term itself comes from the Persian word meaning eyebrow and cloud. One type of EBRU is known as "battal" (or plain). EBRU consists of forms reminiscent of eyebrow and cloud shapes. The materials used in making EBRU are dye (all earthen), kitre (gum tragacanth), od (bile), tekre (trough), firca (brush), combs, wire, paper (almost any kind) and muhre (polishing stone).

EBRU in light colors is used as a background for calligraphy, bookbinding and other forms of art.

In the Mediterranean, names give meaning to the establishment in which they are named. We believe our service and food are quality - just as the Turkish art of EBRU.

We are open seven days a week for breakfast, lunch, dinner, and take home. Enjoy our new early 7:00 AM opening and Friday–Saturday late night 10:30 PM closing with entertainment (free). Come and enjoy our many kinds of baklava, fresh hand-squeezed juices, hot gyro sandwiches, filled pastries, many mouth-watering Mediterranean salads, grocery items and smiling faces to serve you.

forest kebab (orman kebabi)

Heat margarine over medium heat in frying pan. Brown meat and onions until all juices are absorbed. Add salt and water; cover and simmer one hour.

Add carrots after 1 hour, simmer 30 minutes; add potatoes and simmer 40 minutes, or until potatoes are tender. Just before serving sprinkle with thyme. Serve hot with rice.

Serves 4

½ lb lamb, cubed
2 lg potatoes, lg dice
2 carrots, lg dice
2 onions, cut into 8 pcs
2 Tbsp margarine
salt
thyme
1 c water

red bean "pilaki" (barbunya pilakisi)

Serves 4

1½ c dry red beans
½ c olive oil
1 carrot, sliced into rounds
8 cloves garlic, minced
1 Tbsp tomato paste
salt
1 tsp sugar
1 lg onion, chopped
3 c water
1 lemon, sliced

Soak beans overnight in water to cover. Drain. Place beans in large pot and cover with water by about 3". Simmer about 25-30 minutes, until nearly tender.

Heat oil in fry pan over medium heat. Add onions and fry until lightly browned; add carrots, tomato paste, 1 tsp sugar, garlic, salt and about cups water. Bring to a boil; add beans, reduce heat to low and cook until beans are tender; remove from heat and cool.

Serve cold with garnish of lemon slices and parsley.

HYATT REGENCY BELLEVUE

Eques
At Bellevue Plaza Place
900 Bellevue Way
Bellevue, Washington 98004
(206) 462-1234

Eques has established itself as a bright star among Eastside restaurants. The menu offers an ambitious selection of Northwest, Pacific Rim and classical cuisine in the comfortable setting of a private club dining room. Whether you're searching for a quiet breakfast setting, business lunch for ten, or a romantic dinner, Eques is your restaurant.

Spectacular views of the Seattle skyline, majestic Mt Rainier and beautiful Lake Washington compliment the comfort and luxuries offered by the Hyatt Regency Bellevue.

As a self contained world where choices never end, the Bellevue Place complex offers upscale boutiques, an array of cuisines, business services and first class athletic facilities all under one roof.

Bellevue Place, a place for people.

bellevue cobb salad

Mix all ingredients together except lettuces. Place mixture on a bed of the lettuces. Garnish with tomato wedges and cucumber slices.

Serves 1

4 oz mixed lettuces
½ tomato, diced
2 oz bay shrimp
1 oz bacon, cooked & crushed
1 oz bleu cheese, crumbled
¼ avocado, diced
2 oz grilled chicken breast, diced

613 9th Avenue, Seattle, Washington 98104
10116 161st Avenue NE, Redmond, Washington 98052
(206) 881-0929

Entrees, a new concept in the food service-hospitality industry, emphasizes Pacific Rim cuisine. We offer a full restaurant menu including eight different salads, eight seafood entrees, thirteen meat and chicken entrees, fourteen pasta and sauce selections and ten to fourteen desserts. However, we are different because we prepare each order in our kitchens and then deliver it to your home or office.

We have been featured in the *Seattle P-I* and have appeared on KING TV's "Seattle Today" show.

chicken in black bean & garlic sauce

Serves 4

2 lbs boneless chicken, cut into pcs
*2 Tbsp preserved and salted black beans**
2 tsp minced garlic
*1 tsp sesame seed oil**
1 tsp sugar
¼ c vegetable oil
2 Tbsp chopped green onions
¼ c soy sauce

Rinse black beans with water to remove excess salt. Lightly crush beans with a fork.

Combine all ingredients except chicken in a small bowl and mix together. Pour mixture over chicken pieces and allow to marinate at least one half hour.

Spread chicken one layer thick on the bottom of a large shallow heat/microwave resistant dish or skewer onto rods.

Steam fifteen minutes on high heat or microwave on high for three to five minutes (be sure to cover with plastic film prior to microwaving).

Serve plain with vegetables or on steamed rice.

** Black beans are available at Asian markets such as Uwajimaya's. Sesame seed oil is available in most major supermarkets in the Asian section.*

EZELL'S FRIED CHICKEN, INC.

501 23rd Avenue
Seattle, Washington 98122
(206) 324-4141

4216 University Way NE
Seattle, Washington 98105
(206) 548-1455

Ezell's Fried Chicken is a family owned restaurant serving some of the freshest and best food in the nation. The restaurant does catering and delivery is available. Ezell's presently has two locations to serve its loyal patrons.

No reservations are required.

ezell's sweet potato pie

Serves 4 to 8 (1 8" pie)

1 lb yams (about 3 c sliced)
2½ Tbsp butter
½ c sugar
½ c plus 1 Tbsp milk
1 egg yolk
½ tsp cinnamon
¾ tsp nutmeg
8" pie crust

Pie crust:
1 c flour
½ tsp salt
⅓ c shortening
2 to 3 Tbsp water

Peel yams. Cut into ¼" slices. Put potatoes in a saucepan with enough water to cover by at least 1". Bring to boil. Reduce heat to medium-high; continue slow boil for 15 minutes or until tender. Drain. Put hot yams in mixing bowl. With an electric mixer, beat in butter, mixing until melted. Add remaining ingredients, beating well after each ingredient. Pour into prepared pie crust. Bake in a preheated oven at 350° for 1 hour.

Pie crust: Place flour and salt in bowl. Cut in shortening. Sprinkle with 2–3 tablespoons water. Mix just until dough forms a ball. Shape dough into a flat round on a flour-covered board. Roll dough into a 10" circle. Fit into an 8" pie pan. Trim or flute edges.

Grazie

CAFFÈ ITALIANO

2301 N 30th
Tacoma, Washington
(206) 627-0231
CAFFE ITALIANO
16943 Southcenter Parkway
Tukwila, Washington
(206) 575-1606
RISTORANTE & CATERING
3820 124th SE
Bellevue, Washington
(206) 644-1200
Catering: 1 800 788 8572

In a turn-of-the-century building overlooking the bay in Tacoma, Grazie features Northern Italian cuisine presented in a warm, comfortable atmosphere. Menu selections include espresso, antipasto, fresh seafoods, pasta, veal and desserts. Grazie also has a full-service Italian deli, outdoor seating and lounge.

Grazie Cafe, located three blocks from Southcenter Mall, features our antipasti, poultry, pastas and desserts, all served from an entertaining exhibition kitchen. Come and try our Bellevue Ristorante and enjoy the foods that have made us popular.

Catering and banquet facilities are available in Tacoma and Bellevue.

insalata misti

Serves 1

6 - 8 Romaine leaves, chopped
6 - 8 spinach leaves
½ c garbanzo beans
2 oz fennel salami, fine julienne
½ c marinated red onion and leeks
18 - 20 balsamic capers
1 roma tomato, sliced
2 Tbsp Italian parsley, coarsely chopped
8 calamata olives, pitted & halved*

To prepare salad: arrange spinach leaves on chilled plate. Combine all ingredients except roma tomatoes and half of the salami. Toss thoroughly with ¼ c lemon thyme dressing. Garnish with salami, roma tomatoes and a few garbanzo beans.

Red Onion, Leek Marinade:
1 c red onion, very thin julienne
1 c leeks, thinly sliced
¼ c extra virgin olive oil
1 Tbsp balsamic vinegar

Red onion-leek marinade: combine all ingredients and allow to stand for 24 hours.

Lemon Thyme Vinaigrette:
2 c extra virgin olive oil
¾ c red wine vinegar
¼ c balsamic vinegar
3 Tbsp pureed roasted garlic
3 tsp chopped lemon thyme, fresh
4 tsp salt
2 tsp pepper, freshly ground

Lemon-thyme vinaigrette: combine all ingredients. Whisk until thoroughly blended. (Makes 10 - 12 servings, holds very well when refrigerated.)

**To pit calamata olives: place olives on flat surface and press down with fingertips on each with a rolling motion; pits will pop free.*

ravioli al formaggio with broiled roma tomatoes

Serves 1

6 - 8 pcs spinach & cheese ravioli
6 halves roma tomatoes, broiled & chilled
1 oz white wine
3 oz chicken stock
1/2 tsp shallots, pureed
1/2 tsp tarragon, fresh
1 Tbsp butter
1 Tbsp parmesan, grated

Broiled roma tomatoes:
roma tomatoes, halved
olive oil

To prepare broiled roma tomatoes: halve roma tomatoes lengthwise. Rub with olive oil and place on broiler, remove when tomatoes begin to soften. Chill until ready to use.

To prepare ravioli: place saute pan over medium flame, add wine, garlic and shallots. Add chicken stock, tarragon and roma tomatoes, reduce to proper consistency. Cook raviolis. Add raviolis to reduced sauce, toss with hard butter, place on bowl or place. Garnish with parmesan and parsley.

pollo con formaggi

Serves 2

2 whole 8 oz chicken breasts, boneless, skinless
3 oz sun-dried tomatoes, julienned
1 c feta cheese, crumbled
4 Tbsp pine nut butter

Pine Nut Butter:
1 c butter
½ c pine nuts (roasted)
4 - 6 drops tabasco
2 Tbsp garlic, pureed
1 Tbsp Worcestershire sauce
1 Tbsp red wine vinegar
2 Tbsp parsley, chopped coarsely

Make a cut in each side of chicken breasts and fill pockets with feta cheese and sun-dried tomatoes; reserve some feta and tomato for garnish.

Grill chicken over mesquite coals, basting chicken lightly with pine nut butter.

When finished, garnish with feta cheese and strips of sun-dried tomatoes. Serve with penne (pasta) and grilled summer squash.

Pine nut butter: Place roasted pine nuts in a food processor and coarsely grind nuts.

In a mixer combine all remaining ingredients.

The butter is excellent for basting grilled poultry or seafood.

315 South Washington Ave
Kent, Washington
(206) 854-5653

h. d. hotspurs bbq brisket

1 untrimmed brisket of beef
*H.D. Hotspurs BBQ rub**
*H.D. Hotspurs Puyallup Fair Sauce**

Trim fat to ¼". Cover all sides of meat generously with H.D. Hotspurs BBQ Rub. Wrap in plastic wrap and refrigerate for 12 hours.

Put hot coals on sides of barbecue so when brisket is placed on the grill there is no flame directly under the meat. Cook at 225° F. for 8 hours and then at 185° F. for 3 hours. Always make sure your brisket reaches 165° F. Let sit for ten minutes before serving.

Slice brisket. Serve with Puyallup Fair Sauce. Use as entree or for sandwiches.

**H.D. Hotspur's BBQ Rub and Puyallup Fair Sauce are available at local grocery stores or at H.D. Hotspurs restaurant in Kent.*

5300 34th NW
Seattle, Washington 98107
(206) 784-1733

For over ten years, Hiram's has given Seattle the kind of casual elegance in dining that makes for a great meal. The restaurant specializes in a variety of fresh Northwest seafoods and features fresh salmon preparations.

Hiram's, named after Hiram Chittenden, designer of the locks at Shilshole Bay, has a sweeping view of the water and boat traffic, providing entertainment at any time of the day. During nice weather, Hiram's large patio overlooking the water is open for lunch, dinner, Sunday brunch or for cocktails and appetizers.

With the spectacular backdrop of the water, the variety and quality of the menu and the enticement of the patio, Hiram's has established itself as one of Seattle's landmark restaurants.

seared salmon with cilantro sour cream

Serves 4

4 8-oz salmon fillets
¼ c sugar
1 Tbsp fajita seasoning
1 tsp cayenne pepper
1 tsp ground cumin
3 Tbsp vegetable oil
1 c sour cream
¼ c chablis
2 tsp honey
1 tsp lemon juice
½ tsp salt
2 Tbsp chopped cilantro

Combine sugar, fajita seasoning, cayenne pepper and cumin. Put seasoning in a long casserole pan and dredge salmon fillets in the seasoning. Combine sour cream, chablis, honey, lemon juice, salt and cilantro in a small bowl until well blended.

Heat vegetable oil in an electric skillet or saute pan until it begins to smoke. Carefully place salmon fillets into pan. Cook on one side until it begins to brown on the edges.

Carefully turn the salmon fillets and turn heat down to low. Cook until interior temperature of salmon is 120° F.

Serve immediately with sour cream sauce over the top.

mesquite broiled salmon with pesto

Serves 2

2 8-oz salmon fillets
½ c olive oil
½ c salad oil
¼ c minced garlic
⅓ c chopped basil
⅓ c roasted pine nuts
zest of one lemon
salt to taste

In a medium size bowl, add all ingredients together except salmon fillets and pine nuts. Let stand one hour.

Trim salmon fillets to remove any bones or skin which may be present. Chop pine nuts and add to pesto marinade, mix well. Add salmon fillets and let marinate 6 hours under refrigeration, turning salmon fillets over every two hours.

Remove from marinade and grill over mesquite charcoal 3 to 4 minutes on each side. Remove from grill and brush on pesto marinade to taste.

Enjoy!

HIRAM WALKER
& SONS, INC.
KAHLÚA
COMEDY CLUB

kahlúa picadillo filling

¼ c raisins, finely chopped
4 Tbsp Kahlúa
⅓ c finely chopped onion
1 Tbsp vegetable oil
½ canned green chiles, finely chopped
1 Tbsp vinegar
1 tsp salt
⅛ tsp pepper
1 lb ground chuck beef
1 can (16-oz) tomatoes, chopped
⅓ c pine nuts or slivered almonds (optional)

Combine raisins and 3 Tbsp kahlúa; set aside. In non-stick skillet, saute onion in oil until transparent. Add green chiles, 1 Tbsp vinegar, salt and pepper. Add beef and raisin mixture.

Lightly brown beef, breaking up meat as it cooks. Add tomatoes and remaining 1 Tbsp each Kahlúa and vinegar. Bring to boil, then simmer until thickened (about 15 minutes).

Stir in nuts, if desired. Makes about; 3 1/4 cups. Use Kahlúa Picadillo for tacos, tostadas, enchiladas or your favorite Mexican casseroles. For parties, serve with dishes of grated cheese, green onions, chopped fresh tomatoes, shredded lettuce, guacamole, sour cream, taco and tostada shells.

kahlúa cornish game hens

Serves 4

½ c Kahlúa
¼ c fresh orange juice
2 Tbsp fresh lemon juice
½ tsp prepared yellow mustard
¼ tsp paprika
3 Tbsp unsalted butter
4 Cornish game hens, thawed (1 lb 6 oz ea)
salt and pepper
2 thin slices each orange and lemon, halved
1 c seedless grapes
grapes (optional)

Preheat oven to 375° F. In small saucepan, combine Kahlúa with orange and lemon juice, mustard and paprika. Add butter. Bring to boil. Then simmer 1 minute. Remove from heat.

Remove giblets from game hens. Rinse hens in cold water; dry well. Season each cavity with salt and pepper, add a half slice orange and lemon and about 8 grapes. Spoon 1 Tbsp Kahlúa-baste into each cavity. Truss or skewer legs and wings.

Arrange hens, breast-side up, in shallow pan. Brush with Kahlúa-baste and cover birds loosely with foil. Roast in lower third of oven for 30 minutes. Remove foil, brush birds with Kahlúa-baste. Continue cooking about 30 minutes, basting occasionally. If necessary, cover with foil to prevent over-browning.

When done, remove trussing or skewers and keep warm on platter.

To make sauce, remove excess fat from pan; add remaining Kahlúa-baste. Bring to boil, simmer until thickened. Spoon over hens. Garnish, if desired. Serves 4.

kahlúa banana brunch cake

Makes 1 cake

1 cup butter, softened
1½ c granulated sugar
3½ c sifted all-purpose flour
1 c mashed ripe bananas (about 2 med)
½ c Kahlúa
4 lg eggs
¼ c milk
1 Tbsp baking powder
1 tsp baking soda
1 tsp salt
¾ c flaked coconut
¾ c chopped walnuts
sifted powdered sugar (optional)

Grease well 10" tube pan. Preheat oven 350° F.

Cream butter and sugar until fluffy. Beat in flour, ½ cup at a time, with remaining ingredients except coconut and nuts. Beat on low speed until mixture is well blended. On medium speed, beat 2 minutes, scraping bowl as you beat. Stir in coconut and nuts. Turn into prepared pan.

Bake 45 to 50 minutes, or until golden brown. Remove from oven; let stand 10 minutes. Invert on cake rack; remove pan.

When fully cooled, dust with powdered sugar, if desired.

kahlúa fantasy chocolate cheesecake

Serves 12 - 14

1½ c semi-sweet chocolate pieces
¼ c Kahlúa
2 Tbsp butter
2 lg eggs, beaten
⅓ c granutlated sugar
¼ tsp salt
1 c sour cream
2 pkgs (8 oz ea) softened cream cheese, cut in pieces
whipped cream (optional)
chocolate leaves (optional)

Chocolate Crumb Crust:
1⅓ c chocolate wafer crumbs
¼ c softened butter
1 Tbsp granulated sugar

Combine chocolate crumb crust ingredients and press firmly in bottom of 9" springform pan. Preheat oven to 350° F.

In small saucepan, over medium heat, melt chocolate with Kahlúa and butter; stir until smooth. Set aside.

In bowl, combine eggs, sugar, and salt. Add sour cream; blend well.

Add cream cheese to egg mixture; beat until smooth. Gradually blend in chocolate mixture. Turn into prepared crust.

Bake 40 minutes or until filling is barely set in center.

Remove from oven and let stand at room temperature for 1 hour. Then refrigerate several hours or overnight. Garnish if desired.

Italia Imports & Exports, Inc.

8015 24th Avenue NW
Seattle, Washington 98117
(206) 789-1951

Italia Imports & Exports, Inc. is proud to feature Italy's leading desserts. Bindi, since 1946, has been Europe's leading dessert supplier in the foodservice industry.

Caffe Lavazza, Italy's number one original espresso, has one of the most modern and state-of-the-art facilities in the world. The company has been roasting coffee beans since 1889 and is now available in Seattle through Italia Imports & Exports, Inc.

spaghetti al caffe lavazza

Serves 4

2 lbs lean ground beef
2 onions, finely chopped
1 clove garlic, finely chopped
2 c peeled & chopped tomatoes
1 c tomato sauce
¾ c strongly brewed Lavazza coffee
1 c sliced mushrooms
2 Tbsp olive oil
¼ tsp oregano
1 Tbsp fresh basil, chopped
pinch salt
spaghetti
grated parmesan cheese

Heat oil over low heat; add onions and garlic; cook gently so garlic does not brown. Increase heat and add ground beef, cooking until browned.

Add tomatoes, mushrooms, tomato sauce and coffee to ground beef. Simmer 30 minutes, adding water if necessary.

Add oregano, basil, salt and pepper to taste; cook an additional 5 minutes.

Serve over cooked pasta; sprinkle with grated parmesan cheese.

roasted pork al caffe lavazza

Serves 4

4 pork chops
1 Tbsp butter
1 onion, finely chopped
½ c water
4 Tbsp cream
1 Tbsp unbrewed Lavazza coffee, finely ground
cooked rice

Heat butter and 1 Tbsp cream over medium heat. Add onions and cook 3 - 4 minutes; add pork chops and cook 7 - 8 minutes each side. Reduce heat to low and cook for 10 minutes; add salt and pepper to taste.

In small saucepan, combine remaining cream, water and ground coffee until smooth and thoroughly heated.

Remove pork chops from pan and place on warmed serving platter. Spoon cream sauce over each chop. Serve with rice accompaniment.

souffle al caffe lavazza

Serves 6

¾ c milk
6 eggs, separated
1 c powdered sugar
½ c cream of rice
1 pinch salt
2 oz Lavazza espresso

Preheat oven to 350° F. Butter a 1 qt souffle dish; set aside.

Bring milk to a boil. In a large bowl, beat 6 egg yolks with the cream of rice, salt and sugar until thickened. Slowly beat in boiled milk and espresso.

In separate large bowl, beat egg whites until stiff; fold into egg yolk mixture. Gently pour into prepared souffle dish. Bake until puffed and golden; about 20 - 25 minutes. Sprinkle with powdered sugar and serve immediately.

319 East 25th Street
Tacoma, Washington 98421
(206) 272-0170

Over 38 years ago, Mr. and Mrs. John Meaker, with the help of their renowned chefs, developed a seasoning salt from the kitchens of the famous Johnny's Dock Restaurant. Johnny's "Chef-Blended All Purpose Seasoning Salt" was only the beginning of a long tradition of high quality seasonings, sauces, spices and now we are proud to introduce our delicious line of salad dressings. Johnny's salad dressings are made exclusively with canola oil. Remember they are a lot more than just a salad dressing.

All of the ingredients in the following recipes can be purchased at any of your local supermarkets.

spaghetti salad

Serves 8

24 oz cooked thin spaghetti
1½ oz Johnny Salad Elegance
1½ c red wine vinegar
2 cloves garlic, chopped
1 sm bottle Italian dressing
1 sliced red onion
1 green pepper, cubed
1 tomato, cubed

Mix all ingredients together and chill at least two hours before serving.

Johnny's Light Salad Elegance can be substituted for Regular Salad Elegance.

hot chicken caesar salad

Serves 2

2 6-oz boneless chicken breasts
6 oz Johnny's Great Caesar dressing
½ tsp Johnny's Pork & Chicken seasoning
2 oz olive oil
4 oz freshly grated parmesan cheese
2 oz croutons
1 head romaine lettuce

Cut chicken into cubes. Saute in olive oil and Johnny's Pork & Chicken seasoning. Drain pan. Add two ounces of Johnny's Great Caesar Dressing and mix well. Place in large salad bowl and add remaining four ounces of Caesar dressing.

For best results, let marinate in refrigerator for one hour. When ready to eat, warm to desired temperature in microwave or sauce pan. Pour over romaine, toss, place in bowls and add parmesan cheese and croutons.

You can substitute fresh pasta for the romaine lettuce for a delicious variation.

cobb salad

Serves 2

6 c mixed salad greens
1 c diced chicken or turkey
1 sliced avocado
1 diced tomato
½ c blue cheese crumbles
½ to 1 c Johnny's Jamaica Mistake to taste
½ c chopped bacon

Fill salad bowls with mixed salad greens. Add turkey, bacon, avocado slices and tomato. Top with blue cheese crumbles and Johnny's Jamaica Mistake.

THE KALEENKA

A RUSSIAN RESTAURANT

1933 1st Avenue at Virginia Street
Seattle, Washington 98101
(206) 728-1278

Kaleenka is the endearing form of name for a shrub called Kaleenka. Several varieties, some as high as 20 feet, grow throughout Eastern Europe and Russia. Clumps of small white flowers appear in the spring, turning later to small red berries. Kaleenka is well known in folk songs and tales, and is a common decorative motif on lacquered wooden items.

The Kaleenka Restaurant has been open 14 years, featuring the foods of the Russian people - tasty dishes developed through the ages by the country folk. Many of these dishes are regional, from the Ukraine, Georgia, and Uzbekistan, reflecting the tastes of these peoples and the fruits of the lands.

The Kaleenka serves imported beer from Holland, Czechoslovakia and the Ukraine, wines from Hungary, Slovenia, and Portugal, and selected domestic beers and wines.

All dishes and desserts are prepared in the Kaleenka kitchen using ingredients and fresh produce from the Pike Place market. Our chefs have been trained in America and by renowned Russian chefs; your assurance of authentic high quality fare. Ethnic decor, friendly staff, authentic foods and a Slavic ambiance make for a memorable Russian evening.

tabaka

Serves 3

3 whole chicken breasts, boneless
paprika

Marinade:
1 c oil
⅓ c soy sauce
1 tsp parsley
1 clove garlic
1 tsp basil
1 tsp dill
¼ tsp pepper

Tabaka is chicken prepared Georgian style. This was the favorite dish of Joseph Stalin, who was from Georgia. He had a chef whose sole duty was to make this dish. The chicken was cut into halves, the halves pounded flat, marinated several hours, then grilled under a weight. The weight ensures full contact with the cooking surface, promoting rapid cooking and retention of the natural juices.

The Kaleenka uses chicken breasts instead of halves.

To prepare: mix marinade ingredients. Marinate chicken breasts 2 hours or overnight.

Remove chicken from marinade, sprinkle with mild paprika, and cook on a grill for 2 minutes on each side, under a weight, at a medium grill temperature.

Serve hot.

galupsi (cabbage rolls)

Serves 4 (8 rolls)

cabbage, one lg head

Filling:
2 c cooked brown rice
¾ lbs ground beef
¾ c tomato juice
1 Tbsp dill weed
1 Tbsp oil
1 med onion, chopped
¼ tsp ea salt & pepper

Sauce:
2 med onions, chopped
2 c tomato juice
½ c sour cream
2 Tbsp dill weed

Remove the core from the cabbage by cutting around it with a sharp knife. Place the cabbage in the microwave for 3 - 4 minutes, until the outer leaves become soft and pliable. Remove soft outer leaves. Repeat microwaving and removing leaves until eight large leaves are obtained.

For filling: chop and brown one onion. Cool and mix with other filling ingredients. Chop remaining cabbage and add to mix.

Lay a cabbage leaf out on the table. Place 2 heaping Tbsp of filling on the leaf near one edge, fold in the sides and roll into a neat package. Pack tightly, seam down, in a buttered pan and bake 20 to 30 minutes at 300° F.

While rolls are baking, prepare the sauce. Chop and brown 2 medium sized onions, add the other sauce ingredients, and boil 5 minutes. After rolls have baked 20 to 30 minutes, pour the sauce over them and continue baking for another 60 minutes.

piroshky

Serves 8 - 10

Dough:
1½ pkgs dry yeast
¼ c warm water
2 Tbsp sugar
1 tsp salt
1½ c milk
1 egg
¼ c oil or butter
4 to 5 c flour

Filling:
1 med onion, chopped
2 lbs ground round beef
1 clove garlic, minced
salt
pepper

Dissolve yeast in water and let stand 10 minutes. In large bowl, combine flour, sugar and salt. Make a well in flour and add milk, egg, oil and yeast. Combine to make a soft dough. Knead about 10 minutes. Let rise one half hour to one hour.

Brown chopped onion and garlic. In separate pan, brown ground beef. Season with salt, pepper, garlic and onion. Cool meat mixture and remove solidified fat.

Pinch a golf-ball sized piece of dough, flatten with fingers or roll out to ⅛" thickness. Place 2 Tbsp filling in center and bring opposite edges of circle together. Pinch securely. (The traditional shape is a plump center with tapering ends.)

Let piroshkis rise seam side down, 30 minutes. Heat oven to 350° F. Brush with egg and bake until golden brown. The piroshky may also be deep fried.

Karam's

Simply Irresistible Cuisine & A Garlic Lover's Paradise
340 15th Avenue East
Seattle, Washington 98112
(206) 324-2370

Our recipes are unique creations developed in our kitchen. We continue a tradition which cherishes quality and freshness of ingredients and the presentation of good food as a celebration of life.

Try our fresh char-broiled chicken with Karam's Garlic Sauce, which came in First Place at the Bite of Seattle. Our juicy, succulent char-broiled stuffed Kibbeh was also a real hit (First Place again). If you haven't eaten eggplant before or do not think you really like it, take the plunge and give Baba-Ghannouj a try. And Karamage, another new palate-pleasing experience, of fresh homemade goat's milk cream cheese with garlic, mint and oregano, a highly requested appetizer.

We have also taken great care in selecting wines and beers to complement our menu: Chateau Musar from Lebanon, Royal Moghreb from Morocco and Sidi Brahim from Algeria. Beers include Rauchbier (smoked beer) from Bavaria, Germany, Lindemans Kriek, a cherry beer from Belgium, and a great local beer, Pike Place Ale, from Pike Place Brewery at the Public Market. Come experience and enjoy a touch of garlic paradise.

Karam's Garlic Sauce, Tahini Garlic Sauce, Baba Ghannouj and Hummus can be purchased at all Larry's Markets, Rainbow Grocery and QFC on 15th Avenue East and The Central Co-op on 12th Avenue East.

tabbouleh (mint & parsley salad)

Serves 4

*¼ c fine burghul (cracked wheat)**
½ c finely chopped mint or 2 Tbsp dried mint
3 c finely chopped parsley
1 c finely chopped onion
2 c chopped tomato
¾ c extra virgin olive oil
1 c lemon juice (approx 4 lemons)
1 Tbsp salt
¼ tsp pepper
*1 tsp sumac (optional)***

Soak burghul in water for 15 minutes. Drain and press out excess water.

Mix together burghul, onion, salt, pepper and sumac. Add parsley, mint, olive oil, lemon juice and tomato.

Mix thoroughly, adding more lemon juice, salt and pepper as preferred.

Serve over romaine.

**burghul/bulgar - Pacific Foods, 6th Ave. South; can also be found in the cereal or rice section of most groceries.*
***sumac - edible red berries from a variety of the Sumac tree; sharp, somewhat sour flavor; Pacific Foods, 6th Ave. South*

lebanese, turkish or arabic coffee

Serves 2

¾ c water
¾ tsp sugar (optional)
¼ tsp cardamom seeds (optional)
2 heaping tsp powder fine grind coffee, freshly ground (we use Torrefazione Italia Milano blend)

A one-cup racwhe or tanaka (a small long-handled copper, brass or enamel coffee pot)

Bring water to a boil. Add sugar and cardamom. Bring to a boil. Add coffee. Bring to a boil. When foam begins to rise, remove from heat. Stir and return to heat.

Simmer approximately 8 minutes. Stir occasionally.

Remove from heat. Allow grounds to settle. Pour into small serving cups (demitasse are a bit large, but they will do just fine).

When you have finished drinking your coffee, place the saucer on top of the cup, turn it upside down and give it a few whirls. Place the cup at an angle upside down on the saucer. Allow the grounds to dry five minutes. Have fun reading the images which have formed on the side of the cup. This is your fortune!

Larry's Markets

Sausage can be the basis for a flavorful meal that is quick to prepare. Always start with a fresh all-natural product. At Larry's Markets we prepare a variety of fresh all-natural sausages using all fresh spices, minimum amounts of salt, no MSG and no preservatives. We've set high standards for our own sausages and we're proud to carry another selection of sausages from Aidells Sausage Co. which also meets our high standards.

Aidells Sausage Co. is owned and operated by Bruce Aidells, whose painstaking attention to quality is his top priority. Ingredients such as binders, MSG, soy products, fillers and artificial flavors are never used in Aidells sausages. Here's what some critics have said about Aidells:

"Flavorful, gusty links that leave you feeling good." - Eating Well magazine

"Cutting edge cooking in response to current health and diet concerns." - Chicago Tribune

So if it's a quick to fix and flavorful meal you're after, stop by Larry's Markets and choose from Larry's Own sausages or one of the great Aidells sausages.

the piemonte with tomato vinaigrette

Grill the sausages over medium-hot coals for 7 to 10 minutes or pan-fry for approximately 10 minutes until nicely browned and thoroughly heated.

Combine vinaigrette ingredients in bowl and whisk together. Place hot sausage on roll and top with vinaigrette.

Alternatives: Turkey Italians hot or mild. Whiskey Fennel or Creole Hot Sausage.

Serves 4

4 to 6 links Aidells Cooked Chicken & Turkey with Sun-Dried Tomatoes Sausages
1 Larry's Own Baguette, cut for sandwiches, or 4-6 Italian rolls
Vinaigrette:
¾ c ripe, fresh tomatoes
3 Tbsp Larry's Markets balsamic vinegar
⅓ c olive oil
¼ c chopped, fresh basil
2 anchovy fillets, finely chopped
salt & pepper to taste

new mexican sausage rolls

Serves 3

6 Aidell's New Mexico Sausages
6 slices jack cheese
1 can whole mild chiles
6 Larry's Markets flour on corn tortillas
Larry's Markets tomato salsa
6 lime wedges

Grill the sausages over medium-hot coals for 7 to 10 minutes or pan-fry for approximately 10 minutes until nicely browned and thoroughly heated.

Place a tortilla in a pan over medium heat. Add a piece of cheese and a green chile and cook until the cheese is melted. Remove the tortilla. Place a sausage over the cheese, spoon on salsa and roll up. Garnish with fresh lime wedges.

Alternatives: Burmese Curry, Creole Hot or Cajun Andouille Sausage.

P.O. Box 1868
Watsonville, California 95077

Produced in the same Watsonville, California location since 1868, Martinelli's Gold Medal Sparkling Cider and Apple Juice are made from only U.S.-grown, fresh apples and contain absolutely no concentrates, no added water, no preservatives, no sweeteners and no additives of any kind. Winner of more than 50 gold medal awards, Martinelli's is available throughout the U.S. and in several foreign countries. S. Martinelli & Company is celebrating their 125th anniversary this year.

hot mulled cider

1 jug (1.5 liter) Martinelli's Cider
15 whole cloves
10" stick cinnamon
¼ tsp powdered allspice

Add spices to cider and bring to boiling point. Remove from heat and let stand for an hour or more. When ready to serve, reheat and remove the whole spices. This may also be served chilled.

red delicious

Serves 1

4 oz Martinelli's Cider
4 rosehip tea bags
2 oz ginger ale
1 tsp sugar
crushed ice
red apple wedge

Heat Cider and steep the tea in it for 8 to 10 minutes. Allow to cool for 12 to 15 minutes.

Pour tea mixture in a tall glass. Add ginger ale and sugar, stir, and add ice. Garnish with apple wedge.

apple juice a-la-mode

Serves 1

8 oz Martinelli's Sparkling Cider
1 scoop vanilla ice cream
whipped cream
cinnamon to taste
nutmeg

Blend ingredients together, garnish with whipped cream and sprinkle of nutmeg; serve in a glass with wedge of apple (for extra appeal, serve inside cored apples).

820 2nd Avenue
Seattle, Washington 98104
(206) 624-3287

Located in the heart of Seattle's downtown financial and business center. "The Met" is very simply the best steak house in town.

Nobody could describe the experience better than *Seattle Times* restaurant critic John Hinterberger. "A downtown business person's restaurant for lunch which becomes a steak house for dinner - arguably the best in town."

The Metropolitan Grill features dry-cured and 28-day aging of its meat. The beef is carefully broiled over the "iron wood of the world," imported mesquite charcoal, to further enhance its flavor. The sight of a fabulous Porterhouse, Delmonico or Chateaubriand for two never was more appealing or flavorful. And there's always fresh King Salmon, Veal Parmigiana, or extra thick Veal Chops to tempt your taste buds.

While beef is the mainstay of the Met, the lunch menu features the freshest pastas, salads, fish and homemade soups. The dinner menu is enhanced by the latest catch of Northwest Seafood.

Rated one of the Top Ten Steak Houses in the country, the Metropolitan Grill continues to be Seattle's favorite Steak House.

lemon rosemary marinated lamb chops

Strip the rosemary leaves off of the stems and rub the chops with the leaves. Combine all other ingredients except the olive oil. Drizzle in the olive oil while whisking briskly to emulsify. Pour liquid over lamb chops and marinate refrigerated for 24 hours.

Broil to desired doneness.

Serves 4

4 7-oz lamb loin chops
1 lemon zested and juiced
2 sprigs fresh rosemary
2 cloves fresh garlic, chopped
½ c extra virgin olive oil
2 Tbsp cider vinegar

zest: A thin peeling of the yellow part of the lemon peel. (A little tool is available that peels the zest in thin strips in one stroke!)

new york peppercorn steaks

Serves 2

2 16-oz New York steaks
1 c cracked black pepper
2 lbs veal bones
¼ c burgundy
⅓ lb mushrooms
⅓ lb onion
⅓ lb celery
⅓ lb tomatoes
½ sm can green peppercorns
¼ c brandy
pinch cayenne pepper
*2 c brown roux**

**Brown roux: browned mixture of equal parts butter and flour. Used as thickening.*

Place bones, ¼ cup cracked pepper, burgundy, mushrooms, onion, celery, and tomatoes in roasting pan and roast at 350° F. for 3 hours. Add 1 gallon water and cook over low heat for eight hours. Strain.

Reduce stock ⅔ and thicken with brown roux. Finish with brandy and green peppercorns. Add cayenne to taste.

Press cracked black pepper into New York steak. Broil to desired doneness and top with a generous amount of sauce.

tenderloin steak sandwich

Soften butter. Add minced garlic, parsley, green onion and granulated onion to butter and blend thoroughly. Butter kaiser dollar buns. Season tenderloin medallions, to taste. Mesquite broil 1 to 2 minutes per side (preferred rare to medium rare).

Serve hot on Kaiser buns.

Serves 5

1 lb beef tenderloin medallions
5 kaiser dollar-sized buns
1 oz steak seasoning
5 Tbsp grade AA butter
1 tsp fresh minced garlic
½ tsp chopped parsley
½ green onion, minced
½ tsp granulated onion

MILLSTONE®
WHOLE BEAN COFFEES

729 100th Street SE
Everett, Washington 98208
(206) 347-3995

millstone®
java shake®

Blend coffee, syrup, and ice cream in blender until smooth. For best results, pour into chilled glasses, let stand a minute. Top with whipped cream and serve.

Makes 2 tall or 4 short shakes

1 c Millstone Bed & Breakfast Blend®coffee (brewed double-strength and chilled)
3 Tbsp chocolate syrup (or add to taste)
5 c vanilla ice cream

millstone® java cooler™ float

Place two large scoops of French vanilla ice cream in a tall frosty glass.

Pour your favorite flavor of Java Cooler over ice cream and enjoy!

Serves 1

2 lg scoops French vanilla ice cream
tall frosty glass
Java Cooler, any flavor

chocolate espresso cake

Makes 1 cake

4 oz semi-sweet chocolate chips
3 eggs, room temperature
¼ c very strong Millstone Northwest Espresso™ or Cafe Europa™
1½ c flour
½ tsp baking powder
1¾ c light brown sugar
1 Tbsp vanilla extract
¾ c buttermilk
½ tsp baking soda
1 c unsalted butter

Preheat oven to 350° F. Butter a 10" springform cake pan. Line bottom with parchment paper, butter, then flour pan.

Make espresso, set aside.

Melt chocolate in a double boiler until smooth; cool. In a large mixing bowl, cream butter. Slowly add in brown sugar. Beat until light and fluffy, about 8 minutes. Add eggs, one at a time. Add melted chocolate. Add vanilla.

Mix cooled espresso into buttermilk. In a separate bowl, sift together the flour, baking soda and baking powder. Starting with the buttermilk, alternately add buttermilk and flour mixtures to batter. Mix each addition well.

Pour mixture into prepared pan. Bake about one hour.

Cool and serve with chocolate frosting and raspberry garnish.

Chocolate Espresso Cake recipe courtesy of Krups.

92 Madison
Seattle, Washington 98104
(206) 624-3646

The Painted Table opened in April 1992 in the Alexis Hotel at 92 Madison Street in downtown Seattle.

The Painted Table prepares their own breads, such as walnut and onion sandwich bread, as well as their own ice creams and granitas.

The menu is seasonal and many of the items are purchased from small vendors and farms, such as Willy Green's Organic Farm in Monroe and Island Meadow Farm and the Country Store Farm on Vashon Island. Executive Chef Emily Moore and her staff supplement their supply of fresh produce from the Pike Place Market.

The Painted Table offers a champagne and sparkling wine bar Thursday through Sunday from 11:00 PM to 1:00 AM. The bar features hand rolled chocolate truffles, fresh seasonal berries and champagne by the glass.

crab cakes painted table

Makes 8 2½ oz cakes

1 lb Dungeness crab meat, picked over
1 sm shallot, peeled & chopped
½ stalk celery, minced
1 lg or 2 sm scallions (green chopped, white minced)
2" pc peeled, seeded and chopped cucumber
1 oz fresh grated fine bread crumbs (one thin slice good white bread)
¼ tsp salt
⅛ tsp white pepper
¼ tsp cayenne pepper
½ tsp Wasabi powder (Japanese horseradish)*
½ tsp lime and lemon zest (or to taste)
1 Tbsp lemon juice
3 to 4 Tbsp orange juice

bechamel sauce:
4 Tbsp butter
4 Tbsp flour
1¼ c warm milk

**Wasabi powder is available at Uwajimaya Grocery in the international district.*

In a large bowl combine all vegetables. Mix in the crab, salt, peppers, zests, citrus juices and fine bread crumbs. Let sit for a few minutes in the refrigerator. Mix in the Wasabi and bechamel. Taste for seasoning and adjust.

Form into cakes about 2½" across and ¾" thick. To cook, heat 1 Tbsp olive oil in flat skillet or griddle until hot, but not smoking. Put in crab cakes and cook until golden brown on both sides. Serve hot with your favorite garnishes.

To prepare bechamel sauce: heat 4 Tbsp butter in a sauce pot until just foaming. Stir in 4 Tbsp flour with a whisk. Cook until bubbly. Pour in 1 1/4 c warm milk and whisk until completely combined (no lumps). Cook over moderate heat, whisking often, until bubbling and thick. Do not let burn on high heat. Pour into a small bowl and cover with plastic to chill.

smoked duck tamales

At the restaurant, we make these tamales with our own cold-smoked duck which we then slowly cook in olive oil and herbs to make a traditional "confit." For easier home preparation, smoked duck or chicken which has been simply roasted and shredded may be used. The filling also uses smoked and roasted garlic, for which you may substitute chopped garlic toasted in olive oil in a skillet till golden brown.

We use fresh masa, which is re-hydrated dried corn, husks removed, ground to a fine dough-like paste. It's available through the Mexican grocery in the Pike Place Market, where you can also get banana leaves and cornhusks for wrapping the tamales.

To prepare filling: toast garlic in olive oil over low heat, stirring occasionally, until very aromatic and golden brown. Remove skin from duck (or chicken) when cooked and shred or chop into small (½") pieces. Chop tomatoes into 1" pieces and mix all ingredients together (including oil) until well-combined. Season with salt if desired and set aside.

To prepare masa: In food processor or bowl of electric mixer, blend together masa and butter until smooth; then add remaining ingredients and blend until smooth. Cover and set aside.

To prepare tamales: mix together sesame seeds and pistachios, put into broad bowl. Lay banana leaf sheet or corn husk on table. Dip

Makes 16 - 24 tamales

Filling:
10 cloves garlic, chopped
¼ c good olive oil
4 roma tomatoes, peeled, seeded & roasted in a 450° oven for 15 minutes
6 oz smoked duck or roasted chicken

Masa:
*1 lb fresh masa**
6 Tbsp butter, softened
1 tsp baking powder
1 tsp salt
1 Tbsp olive oil
1 Tbsp sesame oil
1 Tbsp apple cider vinegar
1 Tbsp orange juice
2 tsp lemon juice
2 dried ancho or California chiles, seeds removed, soaked ½ hr. in hot water to cover, then whirled in blender till smooth*
½ onion, diced & sauteed in olive oil with 2 garlic cloves, chopped
1 tsp salt
3 tsp ground cumin
1 tsp chile flakes

Tamale ingredients:
see following page

smoked duck tamales *continued*

palm of hand into water and spread about 3 Tbsp masa onto palm, making a thick "pad." Place 1 Tbsp filling onto masa; fold masa around filling, using moistened fingers of other hand, forming a rough "log." Turn log out onto pistachio-sesame mixture and roll to cover with seeds and to compact the shape.

Place in center of wrapper and fold wrapper around filling like an envelope. Tie each packet with a strip of banana leaf or corn husk to hold envelope flaps in place. Steam tamales above boiling water for 12 minutes. Serve immediately with your favorite chutney or salsa and sour cream or creme fraiche.

Tamales may be reheated by steaming.

Tamales:
1 c toasted pistachio nuts, chopped fine
½ c sesame seeds, toasted 5 minutes in 350° oven
1 8-oz pkg corn husks, soaked in hot water ½ hour until soft & pliable, and/or
1 pkg banana leaves, boiled in a lg pot of water for ½ hr then drained and cut with scissors into sheets 8"x10"
bowl of warm water for dipping hands while rolling tamales

**masa (Mexican): re-hydrated dried corn, husks removed, ground to a fine, dough-like paste. Available at Mexican grocery, Pike Place Market.*
**smoked duck or chicken breasts (or meat) available at Larry's Markets or Seattle Supersmoke.*

Pizzeria Pagliacci
4529 University Way NE
426 Broadway Ave E
550 Queen Anne Ave N
SeaTac Mall

Pagliacci Delivery Kitchen
55th and University Way NE (University)
40th and Stone Way N (Wallingford)
10th Ave E and Miller Street (N Capitol Hill)
85th and Dibble (Greenwood)

Pagliacci means clown in Italian. Pagliacci serves an East Coast or Neapolitan style pizza. The first Pizzeria Pagliacci opened in the U-District in 1979 and featured "pizza-by-the-slice." The pizzeria was quite popular and led to the opening of additional pizzerias in the greater Seattle area. In 1992, Pagliacci opened its first delivery kitchen in the U-District. Pagliacci currently delivers to most Seattle neighborhoods north of downtown.

Pagliacci is not a chain or a franchise. Our goal isn't to be the biggest but is to be the *best*. Pagliacci has been voted "best pizza" by readers of *Seattle Weekly* since 1986. We hand-spin every pizza dough, we use 100% whole milk mozzarella cheese and we cook the pizza on hot bricks like it's done in Italy.

crosta con pomodoro

Peel cucumber slightly, cut in half, and slice about 1/4". Core tomato and cut into 8 to 12 pieces. Julienne the green pepper. Slice red and white onions thinly into rounds. Chop fresh oregano in medium pieces. Pit and halve calamata olives.

To prepare dressing: toss dressing ingredients and let marinate 2 to 3 hours. Cut pizza dough into serving size wedges, line a serving dish and spoon salad into center of dish. Crumble goat cheese over the top.

Serves 4 to 6

2 cucumbers
1 tomato
2 green peppers
1 sm red onion
1 sm white onion
4 sprigs fresh oregano
10 calamata olives
2 oz goat cheese
2 - 8" pizza doughs, baked

Dressing:
1 c olive oil
¾ c wine vinegar
½ c balsamic vinegar
1 to 2 Tbsp sugar
salt and white pepper to taste

pizza dough centioli

Makes 3 thin or 2 thick crusts

2 c warm water (105-115°)
1 env dry yeast
1 Tbsp salt
2 Tbsp olive oil
5½ c flour (preferably unbleached bread or high-protein)

Pour ¼ cup of the warm water into a measuring cup, sprinkle in yeast and stir to dissolve.

In a large bowl combine the remaining 1¾ cups of warm water, salt, olive oil and 3 cups of the flour and mix well by hand. Add the yeast mixture and gradually work in the remaining 2 ½ cups of flour.

Knead the dough for about 10 minutes. It should be firm, but elastic. Shape into a ball and turn into a greased bowl to coat surface of dough. Cover bowl and put in a warm place, such as an electric oven with the light turned on until doubled in size, about 1 hour.

Knead dough again and then let it rest for about 10 minutes. To form crusts divide the dough into three pieces if you want three 15-inch thin crusts or into two pieces if you want two 15-inch thick crusts.

For a lighter crust, toss the dough in the air a few times, then finish spreading it out with your fingers on greased pans.

Lightly brush dough with olive oil and tomato sauce. If making a thick crust, let it rise about another 30 minutes before topping with your favorite ingredients and cheeses.

Bake pizzas in a preheated 450° F. oven until edges are well-browned and the cheese is bubbly. Watch closely to make sure they do not burn.

speidini alla romana

Serves 2 to 4

½ lb scamorza cheese (molded in a pear shape with cord tied around the narrow top)
1 French baguette of bread
1 c virgin olive oil
2 cloves of minced garlic
2 tsp fresh rosemary, removed from stem and chopped

In the summer this can be slowly grilled and in winter it can be baked in the oven.

Marinate minced garlic and rosemary in olive oil. Cut baguette in half, remove ends. Slice into ¾" thick slices. Cut cheese into slices about ¼" thick.

On 12" skewer, alternate bread with cheese until skewer is filled (beginning and ending with bread). If grilled place on grill and slowly turn until cheese melts. If done in oven place on baking sheet in 400° F. oven. When cheese begins to melt place on serving dish, remove skewer and ladle olive oil over the top.

Elliott Bay Marina
2601 W. Marina Place
Seattle, Washington 98199
(206) 285-1000

Seattle's newest and most exciting waterfront restaurant, located at the foot of Magnolia Bluff, at the Elliott Bay Marina. The Palisade uses four distinctive preparation techniques to cook Pacific Northwest fresh fish, shellfish, and aged meats: the wood fire rotisserie, the applewood broiler, the searing grill and the wood fired oven.

Enjoy a sweeping view of Seattle's skyline, Puget Sound, Mt. Rainier and the Olympics.

scallops with cabernet glaze

Serves 4

2 lbs scallops
2 oz oil
2 tsp seasoning salt
4 oz beurre blanc sauce
2 oz toasted macadamia nuts, chopped
1 Tbsp parsley
2 c cabernet
¼ c sugar
½ tsp lime juice
1 tsp arrowroot powder

Place the cabernet and sugar into a sauce pot and reduce to 25% of original volume. Mix the lime juice and arrowroot together. Mix into the reduced sauce. Let cook until smooth.

Season scallops with salt, spread oil over the searing grill and cook scallops on both sides until just done.

Place the scallops on the plates, sauce with beurre blanc and cabernet reduction. Top with macadamia nuts and parsley.

palisade spring greens with mandarin orange dressing

To prepare Mandarin dressing: in a mixer or blender, combine and blend all ingredients except for the oil until the sugar is dissolved. Slowly drizzle in the oil until well mixed. Refrigerate until needed.

To prepare candied almonds: preheat oven to 500° F. In a small heavy gauge saucepan, combine the sugar and water. Bring to a boil and turn down to a simmer. Simmer 2 to 3 minutes until sugar is completely dissolved (it should be a fairly heavy syrup consistency). Remove from heat.

Measure the sliced almonds evenly into two steel 12" saute pans. Pour half of the syrup into each pan of almonds and fold until almonds are evenly coated.

Place in oven, stir often. As almonds brown, stir more often toward end of cooking. Cook until sugar is caramelized and almonds are toasted (some charring is okay). Transfer candied almonds onto a sheet pan and let cool just enough to handle (almonds should remain warm to the touch). Using fingers, gently separate sliced almonds into tiny clusters.

To serve greens: toss the crisp seasonal greens, celery and green onion with dressing. Garnish with Mandarin orange slices and candied almonds.

Serves 4

12 oz seasonal greens
6 oz Mandarin Salad dressing
2 oz celery, sliced on bias, ⅛" x 2"
1 oz green onions, green & white parts, ⅛" x 1½"
4 oz Mandarin oranges, drained
2 oz candied almonds

Mandarin salad dressing:
1 c Canola oil
½ c white wine vinegar
½ c granulated sugar
2 tsp kosher salt
1 tsp coarse ground black pepper
¼ tsp tabasco

Candied Almonds:
¾ c granulated sugar
¼ c water
5 oz untoasted sliced almonds

3014 3rd Ave N
Seattle, Washington 98109
(206) 284-3000

Ponti Seafood Grill is located on the ship canal just west of the Fremont Bridge in a European-like setting, with views of the Fremont, Aurora, and ship canal bridges. Hence the name ("ponti" means "bridges" in Italian).

Owners Jim Malevitsis and Richard Malia, along with chef Alvin Binuya, created a menu with broad appeal and a wide variety of preparations, taking the best of many different ethnic cuisines.

bronzed salmon sandwich

"Bronzing" is a term we use referring to the method of cooking. It is basically the same as "blackening," but requires a lower temperature, and is not cooked to the point of blackening the outer crust. This allows a slightly more delicate seasoning to allow more of the natural flavors of the fish to come through.

To prepare: blend all seasoning ingredients together. Heat a heavy skillet with peanut oil until it just begins to smoke.

Oil a thinly sliced 3 to 4 oz filet of salmon, and dredge in seasoning mix. Add to heated pan and leave undisturbed for 1 to 2 minutes. Turn over to complete cooking, 2 to 3 minutes.

Prepare each burger bun with favorite tartar sauce, lettuce, tomato, and sliced avocado. Top with salmon.

3 Tbsp salt
6 Tbsp paprika
2 Tbsp onion powder
2 Tbsp garlic powder
2 Tbsp cayenne
1 Tbsp white pepper
1 Tbsp black pepper
2 tsp thyme
2 tsp oregano
1 Tbsp cumin
1 3- or 4-oz salmon filet per person
hamburger or sandwich rolls
lettuce leaves
sliced tomato
sliced avocado
tartar sauce
peanut oil to coat bottom of skillet

ponti thai curry penne

Serves 2

1 Tbsp butter
1 tsp chopped garlic
¼ c diced onion
1 lg granny smith apple, cored & diced
2 tsp curry powder
pinch salt and pepper

1 c Marsala
1 c chicken broth
3 tsp Thai red curry paste
2 tsp Thai fish sauce
1 c coconut milk
1 c whipping cream
½ lb penne pasta
¼ lb Dungeness crab meat
½ c tomato chutney
fresh chopped basil

Tomato chutney:
½ c rice vinegar
1 tsp grated ginger
¼ c brown sugar
2 tsp lemon juice
1 lb can pear tomatoes, drained & chopped
1 stick cinnamon

Combine the first six ingredients in a medium saucepan and saute over high heat until onions are soft.

Add the Marsala to the apple and onion mixture and reduce to half volume. Add chicken broth, curry paste and fish sauce; simmer for 10 minutes. Allow mixture to cool and blend until very fine in a food processor or blender.

Cook pasta according to directions. Drain and set aside. Heat coconut milk, cream, and the curry mixture and cook until thick. Toss the crab meat and pasta into the sauce to coat. Divide onto two plates and top with the tomato chutney and fresh chopped basil if desired.

Tomato chutney: combine vinegar, ginger, brown sugar and lemon juice and simmer 5 minutes. Add chopped pear tomatoes and cinnamon stick and simmer 30 minutes.

2201 First Avenue
Seattle, Washington 98121
(206) 443-0975

crawfish etouffé

Combine ingredients of spice mix in small bowl and set aside.

Saute mirepoix vegetables in a little butter until slightly softened. Remove from heat and set aside.

Combine ingredients for sauce in saucepan. Simmer for 15 to 20 minutes. Remove from heat.

Prepare roux in large saucepan or small stockpot: heat oil until flour will dissolve upon contact. Slowly add flour, stirring constantly. Stir continuously as mixture begins to change color from hazelnut to medium reddish-brown. (If black specks appear in the roux, it has been scorched and you must begin again.) When desired color is reached, remove from heat and add mirepoix. Stir in thoroughly.

Slowly add sauce mixture to roux, stirring constantly, over low heat until thickened.

Melt butter in large saucepan. Saute crawfish meat for 5 minutes. Add green onions. Add the sauce mixture and simmer until reduced to desired thickness (won't run off the plate).

Serve with 1 cup rice for entree or ½ to ¾ c rice for appetizer.

Serves 6 to 8 as main course;
10 to 12 as appetizer

3 lbs crawfish meat
3 oz unsalted butter
1 c green onions, chopped
8 c long grain or basmati rice, cooked

roux:
1 c olive oil
1 c flour

mirepoix:
2 c celery, finely chopped
2 c onions, finely chopped
2 c peppers, finely chopped (this can be 100% bell peppers or a mixture of chilis, depending on desired hotness)
¼ c garlic, finely chopped

sauce:
8 c seafood stock
2 c canned tomatoes, pureed in processor
1 c heavy cream
¼ c lemon juice
2 Tbsp tabasco

spice mix:
1 Tbsp salt
1 Tbsp white pepper
1 Tbsp black pepper
1 Tbsp dried basil
2 tsp red pepper
1 tsp ground clove
1 tsp paprika

Raga

CUISINE OF INDIA

555 108th Ave NE
Bellevue, Washington 98004
(206) 450-0336

chicken tikka (tandoori chicken tikka)

Cut chicken into 1½" x 1½" cubes.

Combine yogurt, cream, spices, garlic, ginger, vinegar, lemon juice and food color in bowl and mix well. Add chicken; cover and marinate at least 4 hours or overnight in refrigerator.

Remove chicken from marinade; pat dry and place chicken cubes on skewers. Broil over coals or under broiler 7 to 10 minutes.

Serve with rice or naan.*

Note: if using bamboo type skewers, pre-soak in water for about 30 minutes.

Serves 4

1 lb skinless, boneless, chicken breasts
⅔ c yogurt
1 oz heavy cream
1 tsp ground pepper
*1 tsp garam masala**
3 cloves garlic, mashed
1 sm pc ginger, mashed
1 Tbsp white vinegar
1 Tbsp lemon juice
salt to taste
¾ tsp red food color

**Garam Masala: blend of dried spices combined and ground together in the home for use as seasoning (curry powder).*
**Naan: flat bread shaped somewhat like a teardrop and traditionally baked in a tandoor oven.*

eggplant bhartha

Serves 2

1 eggplant, whole
2 onions, sm dice
2 tomatoes, sm dice
1 tsp paprika
¼ tsp turmeric
1 tsp garam masala
4 tsp vegetable oil
2 Tbsp coriander leaves, chopped (cilantro)

Pre-heat oven to 400° F. Place eggplant in shallow baking pan and bake until soft. Remove and cool until easily handled. Peel eggplant under running water. Place eggplant in bowl and mash. Set aside.

Heat vegetable oil in fry pan over medium heat. Add onions and saute 5 minutes; add tumeric and cook 5 minutes, Add tomatoes, paprika and mashed eggplant. Reduce heat to low and cook until lightly browned, stirring occasionally.

Sprinkle with garam masala and chopped coriander leaves. Serve hot.

102 Cherry Street
Seattle, Washington
(206) 343-9517

farafalle orto mare

Serves 4

1 box farafalle (bowtie pasta)
32 Manila clams (approx., 8 per person
½ c + 2 Tbsp olive ol
2 cloves garlic, thinly sliced
2 Tbsp fresh sage, minced
2 Tbsp fresh basil, minced
2 sm zucchini, sliced paper thin
salt, pepper to taste

Bring water to boil for pasta. Add 1 Tbsp oil and salt to the water. Cook pasta until done. Drain and set aside.

In large pan heat half of olive oil, add half of garlic and clams and saute until clams open. Reserve clam juice.

Remove clams from pan. Saute the zucchini in 1 Tbsp olive oil until lightly browned; add basil and sage.

In large saute pan, heat remaining ½ c oil, remaining garlic. Add clams, clam juice, zucchini and pasta; toss together thoroughly. Add salt and pepper to taste. Serve hot!

279 Madison Ave N.
Bainbridge Island, Washington 98110
(206) 842-1999

San Carlos Restaurant, last year's winner of the Bite of Seattle's "Best Entree Award," is proud to celebrate nine years of serving the Northwest.

San Carlos Restaurant is located on Bainbridge Island, and is a 35 minute ferry ride out of the downtown Coleman terminal. You may walk on the ferry, as the San Carlos is about 5 blocks from the Bainbridge Terminal, or bring the car, bicycle, motorcycle, etc.

What a delightful way to spend a summer's afternoon or entertain guests, by traveling Puget Sound, then rewarding yourself with an award-winning dinner from the Northwest's first Southwestern restaurant.

San Carlos was also named "Best Restaurant in Kitsap County" by the Tidelands Publishing Group (1986), and won the "Best Appetizer" award at the 1991 Taste of Edmonds.

We are open for dinner daily at 5:00 P.M. and serve luncheon on Fridays only. Please call for reservations.

herbed crab chimichanga

Serves 8
Winner 1992 Bite of Seattle "Best Entree" award

2 lbs Dungeness crab
¾ c cream cheese
½ c shrimp stock
1 c kernel corn
½ c diced onion
½ c diced red & green bell pepper
1 lemon
1 bunch cilantro
2 Tbsp fresh Anaheim chili powder
pinch salt, pureed garlic, fresh dill, oregano & white pepper
1 qt vegetable oil
1 doz med flour tortillas
1 lb grated cheddar cheese
1 pint sour cream (optional)
1 lg tomato, diced

In a saucepan, combine shrimp stock and cream cheese and heat until creamy. Combine in mixing bowl with Dungeness crab.

Lightly saute onion and pepper just enough to an *al dente* crunchiness and add to mixing bowl. Lightly saute kernel corn, chili powder, salt, white pepper and pureed garlic in 2 Tbsp butter and add to mixing bowl. Add fresh dill (chopped), oregano, ⅓ bunch of cilantro (chopped) and juice of lemon to taste.

After thoroughly mixing above ingredients, keep warm until ready to serve, about 1 hour.

On a grill or heated surface (i.e., Teflon saucepan, 10"), warm tortillas until pliable. Then lay tortilla flat and place about 3 Tbsp of crab mixture and grated cheddar cheese in center of tortilla. Fold sides of tortilla over, then starting closest to you, fold tortilla over mixture and roll into a small burrito, approximately 4 to 5" long and 2½" wide. (Tip: chimichanga must be tightly rolled or it will leak and come apart in vegetable oil.) Repeat until all tortillas have been filled.

Heat vegetable oil to 350°, and carefully lay chimichanga into pan. Flash fry until golden brown on all side. Remove and hold on any kind of tray over paper towel until ready to serve.

Serve with cream salsa sauce (recipe follows) and garnish with fresh cilantro leaves, sour cream (and guacamole if you like), diced tomatoes, crab legs and lemon wedge.

cream salsa sauce

Serves 8

salsa fresca, 1 pint
½ pint sour cream
½ pint mayonnaise
½ c buttermilk
pinch salt
pinch granulated garlic

Salsa Fresca:
6 fresh tomatoes
1½ c tomato sauce
2 Tbsp salt
1 to 1½ Tbsp garlic, minced or pureed
2 Tbsp ground cumin
2 sm yellow onions
1 c fresh cilantro
½ c jalapeno or serrano chilis

Mix ingredients in an appropriate size mixing bowl. Season to taste with salt and granulated sugar.

Spoon 1½ to 2 oz over crab chimichanga, then add remaining garnishes (crab legs, cilantro, diced tomato, olive slices, onion slices, guacamole, etc.) to your taste, and in an aesthetically pleasing display for the eye.

This sauce will add a smooth, rich salsa flavor to your award-winning chimichanga, and can also be used as a dip for vegetables, cheese or crackers, and with a touch of balsamic vinegar becomes a very interesting salad dressing.

To prepare Salsa Fresca: wash, stem and dice tomatoes. Load into blender or food processor. Add ½ cup water and tomato sauce. *Very briefly* blend just until liquefied. *Do not overblend.* Place the mixture in a two quart container.

Peel the onions. Mince one onion and add to the salsa. Place the other onion whole in a blender bowl and add ½ cup water, salt, cumin, and garlic. Blend thoroughly and add to salsa mixture.

Chop 1 cup of loose cilantro (leaves only) and add to salsa mixture. Mince chilis and add to salsa mixture. Stir salsa to combine.

This is a recipe for a basic salsa cruda. It will refrigerate for 10 days to 2 weeks, and is one of the basics for good Southwestern cooking.

yucatan grilled chicken with san carlos black beans

Serves 6 to 8

2 lbs boneless, skinless chicken thighs or breasts
*1 4-oz pkg achiote**
2 c pork stock
2 c chicken stock
salt to taste
pureed garlic to taste
2 lbs black beans
1 med yellow onion
salt to taste (approx 1 tsp)
2 to 3 tsp pureed garlic
1 sm smoked ham hock

Add black beans to 10 quart pot and add 5 quarts water (or chicken stock if available). Add chopped onion, salt, garlic and ham hock and bring to a boil. Reduce heat and simmer for at least 3 hours. The longer you simmer the better the beans. You may need to add additional liquid to keep beans fluid, and stir occasionally to prevent sticking.

While beans are simmering, crumble achiote and mix with stocks, bring to boil, reduce heat and simmer for about an hour. Sauce should have some substance but not be too thick.

Dip chicken in achiote sauce and marinate for 1 to 2 hours (or longer if possible).

Grill chicken over mesquite charcoal.

Serve grilled chicken with the black beans, spooning a little of the warmed sauce over chicken and beans if desired. Garnish with fresh cilantro, guacamole, sliced jalapenos, pepper jack cheese etc.

**Achiote: Brick-red seeds (also called annatto seeds) ground to make a paste with chili powder, herbs and spices; from the Yucatan Peninsula. Available at any Larry's Market or Mexican specialty market such as La Tienda in the Pike Place Market.*

BLACK ANGUS RESTAURANT
20102 44th Avenue West
Lynnwood, Washington 98043
(206) 774-6556

Stuart Anderson's Black Angus Restaurant has been serving fine steaks, chicken, and seafood all over the Seattle area for 25 years.

Convenient locations in Lynnwood, Renton, Everett, and Crossroads. Open seven days a week.

caribbean chicken

Serves 1

1 4½-oz chicken breast
2 oz Caribbean Marinade
1 oz Caribbean Sauce

Caribbean Sauce:
(makes approx. 1 qt.)
1¼ oz garlic, minced
2¼ c brown sugar
2 c red wine vinegar
1 Tbsp chicken base
1 c ketchup
¾ oz corn starch
1 oz water
4 Tbsp orange juice

Marinate chicken breast in Caribbean Marinade for 24 hours. Remove chicken and pre-heat broiler. Discard marinade.

Broil chicken until done. Place on plate. Ladle some sauce over chicken. Serve with french fries and fruit salad.

To prepare Caribbean Sauce: combine first five ingredients and mix well. Bring to a boil. Boil 8 minutes. Reduce to simmer.

Whisk together remaining ingredients until smooth. Gradually add to the simmering mixture. Simmer until clear and thickened.

chicken papaya salad

Toss carrots, peppers, sliced lettuce, mushrooms and 1½ oz dressing.

Arrange romaine leaves on large glass salad plate. Mound salad mix in center. Slice chicken into 12 pieces and arrange on top of salad. Cut peeled and seeded papaya into eighths. Arrange 3 papaya wedges and 3 tomato wedges around salad. Pour 1 oz dressing across chicken slices.

Sweet & Sour Ginger Dressing: sift sugar and dry mustard together into double boiler. Add vinegar to sugar mixture. Cook until sugar dissolves.

Gradually stir in remaining ingredients in order listed. Remove from heat. Refrigerate overnight. Stir well before using.

Serves 1

2 oz carrots, 2" matchsticks
2 oz red bell peppers, 2" matchsticks
3 oz romaine lettuce, sliced ½" wide
2 oz sliced mushrooms
1½ oz Sweet & Sour Ginger dressing
3 ea romaine leaves
1 grilled chicken breast
3 tomato wedges
⅓ papaya, peeled & seeded
1 oz Sweet & Sour Ginger Dressing

Sweet & Sour Ginger Dressing:
(makes approx. 1 qt.)
2 c sugar
4 tsp dry mustard
1 ½ c white vinegar
2 Tbsp soy sauce
2 tsp ginger, fresh, peeled & grated
1 tsp garlic, minced
¼ c vegetable oil
2 Tbsp sesame oil
2 tsp black pepper
1½ tsp salt
1 Tbsp lemon juice

1122 Post Ave
Seattle, Washington 98101
(206) 467-8226

In the heart of the Seattle waterfront neighborhood on the corner of Seneca and Post, lies Tlaquepaque Bar and Restaurant. Live mariachis, the original tequila "popper," and the only authentic Mexican cuisine in the Northwest make Tlaquepaque a one-of-a-kind experience. Our original, award-winning entrees have captured the attention of Bite of Seattle judges for over eight years. And this year will be no exception. We look forward to seeing you at booth #8 for one of our fabulous empanadas. We hope you can join us downtown for one of our hand-shaven margaritas and our spectacular regional Mexican cuisine. *Salud!*

empanada pastry / flour tortillas

Makes 1 dozen 8" tortillas

2½ oz vegetable shortening
2 Tbsp hot water
1½ lb all-purpose flour
1 tsp salt
1½ tsp baking powder

**empanada: Spanish-style turnover*

Sift all dry ingredients together. Add water and shortening. Mix on medium with dough hook until dough forms a ball. Divide the dough into 12 equal portions and let stand for ten minutes in warm place. Roll out very thin, into 8" circles.

For tortillas: grill immediately on hot, flat grill or fry pan for about 6 minutes.

To prepare empanadas: brush tortilla with beaten egg. Place 3 oz filling on one-half of round; fold over into half moon shape and pinch edges to seal. Brush pastry with egg and puncture top of pastry with a fork. Bake at 350° F. for 15 minutes.

seafood empanada

Makes 1 dozen empanadas

1 recipe of pastry dough
2 c cream sauce
1½ lbs seafood (your choice)
1 med onion, diced
1 c celery, diced
salt & pepper to taste
2 Tbsp butter
¼ c chopped cilantro
1 egg, beaten

Saute vegetables and cilantro in butter with seasonings. Add seafood and cook until seafood is done. Remove from heat and cool.

Stir cream sauce into seafood mixture. Fill pastry with seafood mixture. (See preceding pastry recipe.) Bake at 350° F. for 15 minutes.

chorizo empanada

Makes 1 dozen empanadas

1 recipe of pastry dough
*2 lbs chorizo**
1 med onion, diced
1 med green bell pepper, diced
2 lg tomatoes, diced
¼ lb cheddar cheese
¼ lb monterey jack cheese
2 eggs, beaten
¼ lb feta cheese
½ pint salsa

Fry chorizo; drain grease. Add vegetables to chorizo and saute until vegetables are tender. Remove from heat and toss in the cheese.

Fill pastry with chorizo filling (3 oz). Bake at 350° F. for 15 minutes.

Serve with crumbled feta cheese and salsa.

**chorizo: Mexican-style sausage (mild to spicy). Do not buy Spanish style for this recipe.*

vegetarian empanada

Makes 1 dozen empanadas

1 recipe of pastry dough
½ lb yellow squash
½ lb zucchini squash
½ lb red bell peppers
¼ lb onions
¼ lb cheddar cheese
¼ lb monterey jack cheese
1 Tbsp minced garlic
salt & pepper to taste
¼ lb feta cheese
½ pint salsa

Saute all vegetables in 1 Tbsp olive oil and 1 Tbsp butter. Remove from heat and toss in grated cheeses.

Fill pastry with vegetable filling. Bake at 350° F. for 15 minutes. Serve with crumbled feta cheese and salsa.

Red Lion Hotel Bellevue
300 112th Avenue SE
Bellevue, Washington 98004
(206) 450-4154

Colorful Italian cuisine in a fun setting is our specialty. At Velato's, we recommend that you start your dining experience with a platter of seasonal antipasti items created especially for you by your server.

Enjoy unique presentations of pasta, seafood and other Northwest regional favorites with an Italian flair.

smoked salmon ravioli with tomato basil cream sauce

Serves 4

20 salmon ravioli (set aside)
1 med white onion
3 minced shallots
1 #303 can diced tomatoes
2 oz chopped garlic
1 oz fresh chopped basil
½ c white wine
¼ c olive oil
1 qt half-and-half, warmed
roux to thicken

In olive oil, saute the first five vegetable ingredients just until tender. Do not overcook. Deglaze with white wine, and let reduce for two minutes. Start to bring small amount of roux into the sauteed mixture, add warmed half and half; finish thickening with the roux to the consistency of a light sauce.

Bring to a boil three quarts of water, a pinch of salt, and 1/4 c of olive oil. When the water is at a full boil add the ravioli one at a time, stir gently, cooking just until tender. Strain the ravioli, then add sauce to the salmon ravioli. Garnish with fresh basil leaf.

tiramisú

Serves 6

3 egg yolks
3 Tbsp superfine sugar
1⅓ c Marasala or brandy
¼ c very strong espresso coffee
8 oz mascarpone cheese, room temperature
½ c heavy cream
1 egg white
4 oz savoiardi or ladyfingers
powdered sugar
cocoa

Tiramisú ("pick me up") is a modern version of a dessert first created in Siena, where it was called zuppa del Duca (the Duke's Soup). From there it migrated to Florence, where it became very popular in the nineteenth century among the many English people who came to live in the city at that time. And so it was called zuppa inglese - English soup. Only recently, the same dessert with some variation - chiefly the substitution of rich mascarpone cheese for the original custard - has come to be called Tiramisú.

Make a zabaglione by beating the egg yolks and sugar in the top of a double broiler until ivory colored. Add ⅓ cup liquor and whisk over gently simmering water until the mixture begins to thicken. Let cool.

Stir the coffee into the mascarpone. Whip the cream to soft peaks. Beat the egg white until stiff. Fold the egg white into the zabaglione and half the cream.

Line the bottom of a 2 quart serving dish with one layer of ladyfingers; sprinkle with half the remaining marsala and espresso. Cover ladyfingers with half each of the cheese and the zabaglione mixtures. Repeat the layers, finishing with the remaining whipped cream.

Refrigerate for several hours before serving. Dust top with cocoa and powdered sugar just before serving.

VIC & MICK'S
NINE-10 CAFE KITCHEN

999 Third Avenue
Seattle, Washington 98104
(206) 622-3999

There are many reasons why Vic & Mick's NINE-10 Cafe has become a reality, but none more important than our desire to serve those whose past and present patronage is the very reason for our existence.

Like virtue, catering to a community's appetite is its own reward. Doing so, in a manner that earns your approval, is the ultimate measure of success. Our hospitality is predicated on the belief that every successful meal requires guests who know what they want, a chef who knows how to prepare it and a manager who understands the meaning of service. Through this blend of understanding we work to make your dining experience most rewarding for all concerned.

For your convenience we have prepared a balanced, simplified permanent menu. We welcome your suggestions and invite you to make this restaurant your home-away-from-home. It will be our pleasure to see that every reasonable demand is satisfied.

semi-freddo torte

Makes 1 cake

1 sm pkg pudding mix
1 c whipping cream
1 cup half-and-half
1 lb cake, loaf size, sliced horizontally, 3 layers
½ to 1 lb semi-sweet chocolate, finely chopped
½ c rum
½ c brandy
1 c anisette
powdered sugar
cocoa

Combine vanilla pudding mix with whipping cream and half-and-half and mix according to package directions. Add finely chopped chocolate.

Combine rum, brandy, and anisette.

Place first layer of cake on serving plate, soak with ⅓ liquor mix. Spread pudding mixture on cake (approximately ½" layer). Repeat layers of pound cake, liquor mix, pudding mixture.

Sprinkle top with mix of powdered sugar and coca. Refrigerate at least four hours.

veal scallopine

Serves 4

4 3 to 3½ oz veal scallops
1 oz oil
1½ oz butter
½ c all-purpose flour
½ tsp salt
5 to 6 grinds fresh pepper
one lemon
1 oz white wine
1 Tbsp capers

Place veal between sheets of plastic. Pound gently. Dust veal lightly with flour. Season with salt and pepper.

Heat oil over medium-high heat in a heavy frying pan. Brown veal quickly on each side. Transfer veal to heated serving dish.

Drain oil from pan. Deglaze pan with wine (1 to 2 minutes). Add veal, butter, capers, and lemon, cut in half, juice squeezed over veal, dropping lemon halves into pan. Cook until sauce thickens.

Turn heat to low, basting veal with sauce once or twice. Discard lemon halves.

Transfer to serving dish and serve immediately.

from the Kitchens
of
I.P.I. Publishing

jood's famous mostaccioli and broccoli

Serves 2

2 c broccoli florets
2 Tbsp olive oil
2 Tbsp butter
2 cloves garlic, minced
salt
pepper
½ c grated pecorino or parmesan cheese
3 handsful mostaccioli

While cooking pasta, saute broccoli and garlic in the butter/oil until crisp/tender. Add salt and pepper to taste.

Drain noodles. Place in large bowl. Toss with the sauteed broccoli and garlic. Top with grated pecorino cheese.

jood's famous beef & broccoli

Serves 2

1 med size tenderloin cut into small strips
2 c broccoli florets
1 can cream of broccoli soup
¼ c water
2 cloves garlic, minced
salt
pepper
2 Tbsp olive oil
¾ of 1 bag wide egg noodles

While cooking pasta, saute tenderloin strips, broccoli and garlic in olive oil. Salt and pepper to taste.

Stir in 1 can broccoli soup and ¼ cup water. Simmer for 5 to 8 minutes. Pour over egg noodles.

erynn's vegetarian lasagne

Serves 8 to 10

1 med eggplant
1 med zucchini, ¼" dice
½ lg onion, chopped
2 cloves garlic, minced
1 lg can tomatoes, coarsely chopped
2 Tbsp olive oil
1 pt ricotta
milk
1 c grated parmesan
2 eggs
8 oz mozzarella, thinly sliced or grated
¼ c parsley, chopped
pinch of nutmeg
pepper to tastre
1 tsp oregano
salt
lasagne dry noodles (about ½ to ⅔ of a pkg), or fresh lasagne noodles or sheets, about 1 lb

Slice eggplant in half lengthwise; slice each half into ⅛" thick rounds. Place eggplant in colander and salt liberally; set aside to drain. In separate colander do the same with the zucchini.

Heat oil in large skillet over medium heat. When oil is hot add onions and garlic; saute until onions are softened, about 5 minutes. Add oregano and pepper to taste. Add tomatoes and their juice; reduce heat and simmer uncovered until thickened.

Bring water to a boil for noodles (if using fresh pasta do not cook noodles as they will cook during baking). Cook dry noodles until just *al dente*. Drain and separate noodles.

In a medium size bowl, beat together ricotta and eggs until smooth. Gradually add milk until thinned to a sauce-like consistency. Stir in parsley, nutmeg and ¼ c parmesan.

Assembly: use a 9" x 13" x 2½" pan. Pat dry eggplant and zucchini. Ladle a little of the tomato sauce into the pan to coat the bottom. Line bottom of the pan with noodles - do not overlap. Place a layer of eggplant slices on noodles. Sprinkle zucchini cubes over eggplant. Spread some of the ricotta mixture over vegetables; cover lightly with tomato sauce, dot with mozzarella and sprinkle on some of the parmesan. Repeat process (there should be three layers) until noodles form last layer. Top with remaining tomato sauce, mozzarella and parmesan.

Bake at 350° F. for about 45 minutes. Let stand 10 to 15 minutes before cutting and serving.

steak & asparagus salad

Combine marinade ingredients in bowl. Add steak strips. Marinate 30 to 60 minutes.

Combine salad dressing ingredients in a jar and heat in microwave about 15 seconds. Cover jar and shake dressing to combine.

Divide salad greens among 4 plates. Arrange asparagus spears and tomato wedges over greens in spoke-like pattern.

Remove steak from marinade and stir-fry in hot skillet 2 to 3 minutes or until desired doneness. Place steak strips in center of each salad. Drizzle salad dressing over each salad and sprinkle with sesame seeds.

Serves 4

¾ lb beef steak, cut across the grain in thin strips
mixed salad greens for 4 people
16 asparagus spears, blanched & chilled
16 tomato wedges
sesame seeds, toasted

Marinade:
3 Tbsp soy sauce
2 Tbsp Balsamic or wine vinegar
1 tsp lime zest
1 sm clove garlic, minced
½ tsp ginger, minced
½ tsp ground pepper

Salad dressing:
1 Tbsp honey
1 Tbsp dijon mustard
2 Tbsp Balsamic or wine vinegar
2 tsp soy sauce
5 Tbsp vegetable oil

boat spaghetti with bay scallops

Serves 4

1 lb fresh bay scallops
1 Tbsp olive oil
1 Tbsp butter
2 roma tomatoes, chopped
¼ c chopped onion
1 garlic clove, minced
*4 Tbsp crême fraiche**
2 Tbsp chopped parsley
2 Tbsp grated pecorino romano cheese
freshly ground pepper
pinch of salt
1 lb thin spaghetti

Bring water to boil for spaghetti. Heat oil and butter in 10" saute pan over medium heat. Add onion and garlic; saute 2 to 3 minutes.

When water comes to boil add spaghetti.

Raise heat in saute pan to medium-high and add scallops to onions and garlic; saute quickly so as not to overcook. Add chopped tomatoes, salt and pepper and cook 1 to 2 minutes. Reduce heat to low. Add parsley and crême fraiche. Stir thoroughly. Simmer until spaghetti is done and sauce is slightly thickened.

Drain spaghetti and place in heated serving bowl. Pour scallops and sauce over spaghetti and toss to coat noodles. Add 2 Tbsp cheese, toss quickly and serve.

**I have found crême fraiche at QFC. It is made by Altadeena Dairies.*

pasta with pepperoncini & ham

Serves 2 to 4

6 med size pepperoncini, coarsely chopped
3 slices Black Forest-style ham, cut in ¼" wide strips
½ red bell pepper, cut into ¼" strips
8 quartered artichoke hearts (packed in water), cut into bite-size pcs
4 cloves garlic, minced
¼ c olive oil
½ c cream
about 5 handsful radiatore pasta

Heat oil in large skillet over medium heat. Saute garlic 2 to 3 minutes. Add red peppers; cook 3 to 4 minutes. Add pepperoncini, ham and artichokes; cook about 5 minutes, stirring occasionally.

Bring water to boil for pasta; cook until *al dente.*

Add cream to pepperoncini and ham mixture; cook until slightly thickened.

Drain pasta and add to sauce; toss to thoroughly coat pasta.

Served with grated cheese.

index

A

B

C

D

E

Tables of Equivalents

WEIGHTS & MEASURES

60 drops	1 teaspoon
3 teaspoons	1 tablespoon
2 tablespoons	1 liquid ounce
4 tablespoons	¼ cup
16 tablespoons	1 cup
2 cups	1 pint
2 pints	1 quart
4 quarts	1 gallon
8 quarts	1 peck
4 pecks	1 bushel
16 ounces	1 pound

EGG

8 to 10 egg whites	1 cup
10 to 14 egg yolks	1 cup
4 to 6 whole eggs	1 cup

COCOA & CHOCOLATE

For 1 ounce (square) chocolate use
4 tablespoons cocoa and ½ tablespoon fat.

For ¼ cup or 4 tablespoons cocoa use 1 ounce (square) chocolate and omit ½ tablespoon fat.

GENERAL EQUIVALENTS

2 cups solid butter = 1 pound

1 bouillon cube = 1 teaspoon beef extract

1 tablespoon cornstarch = ⅔ tablespoon arrowroot or 1¾ tablespoons wheat or rice flour

1 tablespoon unflavored gelatin = ¼ ounce (or 2⅔ leaves leaf or French gelatin)

FRESH FRUIT

1 pound apples	2 to 6 apples; 3 cups, diced; 1½ cups sauce
1 pound apricots	8 to 14 apricots; about 2½ cups, cooked
1 medium avocado	about 2 cups, cubed
1 pound bananas	about 3 bananas; about 2 cups, sliced
1 pint berries	about 2 cups
1 pound cherries	3 cups, stemmed; about 2½ cups, pitted
1 pound cranberries	about 4 cups; about 4 cups sauce
1 medium grapefruit	about 1⅓ cups pulp, about 1 cup juice
1 pound grapes	about 1 bunch; about 2 cups, halved
1 dozen lemons	about 2½ cups juice
1 dozen oranges	3 to 5 cups juice
1 pound peaches	4 to 6 peaches; about 2½ cups, sliced
1 pound pears	3 to 5 pears; about 2½ cups, cooked
1 pineapple	about 2½ cups, cubed
1 pound plums	12 to 20 plums; about 2 cups, cooked
1 pound rhubarb	4 to 8 stalks; 3½ cups diced; 2 cups, cooked

Kitchen Notes:

I.P.I. Publishing
10245 Main Street, Suite 8-3
Bellevue, Washington 98004
(206) 454-8473

Please send me__________copies of **The Bite of Seattle Cookbook** at $12.95 each (plus $1.04 sales tax [Wash. residents] and $2.00 postage and handling: Total $15.99)

Enclosed is my check for $____________________.

Name____

Address____

City____State__________Zip______________

☐ This is a gift. Send directly to:

Name____

Address____

City____State__________Zip______________

- (Cut Here) --

I.P.I. Publishing
10245 Main Street, Suite 8-3
Bellevue, Washington 98004
(206) 454-8473

Please send me__________copies of **The Bite of Seattle Cookbook** at $12.95 each (plus $1.04 sales tax [Wash. residents] and $2.00 postage and handling: Total $15.99)

Enclosed is my check for $____________________.

Name____

Address____

City____State__________Zip______________

☐ This is a gift. Send directly to:

Name____

Address____

City____State__________Zip______________

Kitchen Notes: